LESSONS IN EXPERIMENTAL AND PRACTICAL GEOMETRY

by

H.S. Hall and F. H. Stevens

YESTERDAY'S CLASSICS

ITHACA, NEW YORK

Cover and arrangement © 2023 Yesterday's Classics, LLC.

This edition, first published in 2023 by Yesterday's Classics, an imprint of Yesterday's Classics, LLC, is an unabridged republication of the text originally published by Macmillan and Co., Limited in 1911. For the complete listing of the books that are published by Yesterday's Classics, please visit www.yesterdaysclassics.com. Yesterday's Classics is the publishing arm of Gateway to the Classics which presents the complete text of hundreds of classic books for children at www.gatewaytotheclassics.com.

ISBN: 978-1-63334-229-3

Yesterday's Classics, LLC
PO Box 339
Ithaca, NY 14851

PREFACE

To give to a young pupil clear mental pictures should be the first object of geometrical teaching: to enable him to express geometrical ideas in the form and order required by strict deductive reasoning is a second and distinct object. Experience shows that these two aims may to some extent be separated with advantage; and accordingly Formal Geometry is now very generally preceded by a short preliminary course of practical and experimental work.

In the preface to our *School Geometry* it is suggested that a suitable introduction to that book would consist of "Easy Exercises in Drawing to illustrate Definitions; Measurements of Lines and Angles; The Use of Compasses and Protractor; Problems on Bisection, Parallels, Perpendiculars; The Use of Set Squares and the Construction of Triangles and Quadrilaterals: these problems to be informally explained, and the results verified by measurement. Concurrently there should be Exercises in Drawing and Measurement designed to lead inductively to the more important Theorems of Part I." It is the purpose of these *Lessons* to supply such an introductory course.

To this scheme we have added very simple chapters on Areas, on Circles and Polygons, and on the Forms of some Solid Figures; but it is not intended that these Sections should necessarily be taken before demonstrative geometry is begun.

This experimental and constructive work should not be allowed to keep a pupil back. He may probably be put to it six months or a year before a start can profitably be made with geometry of a more formal kind; and when the latter stage is reached, his practical knowledge should not only add life and interest to his theoretical work, but greatly accelerate its progress.

In each Section more exercises are provided than Teachers are likely to need for a first course: the rest may be taken afterwards with the corresponding propositions in the *School Geometry*, to which this little book is intended as a supplement as well as an introduction.

H. S. HALL

F. H. STEVENS

December 1904

CONTENTS

I. SOLIDS, SURFACES, LINES 1

II. MEASUREMENT OF STRAIGHT LINES .. 8

III. STRAIGHT LINES CONTINUED 15

IV. CIRCLES 19

V. ANGLES 26

VI. ANGLES CONTINUED 38

VII. DIRECTION, PARALLELS 44

VIII. PERPENDICULARS 55

IX. TRIANGLES 65

X. TRIANGLES CONTINUED: CONGRUENCE AND PRACTICAL APPLICATIONS 74

XI. QUADRILATERALS 83

XII. AREAS 91

XIII. MISCELLANEOUS CONSTRUCTIONS, CIRCLES, REGULAR POLYGONS 104

XIV. THE FORM OF SOME SOLID FIGURES 114

ANSWERS 125

NECESSARY INSTRUMENTS

THE pupil should be provided with the following instruments and apparatus:

1. A flat ruler, one edge being graduated in centimetres and millimetres, and the other in inches and tenths.

2. Two set squares; one with angles of 45°, and the other with angles of 60° and 30°.

3. A pair of pencil compasses.

4. A pair of dividers, preferably with screw adjustment.

5. A semi-circular protractor.

The instruments referred to above in Nos. 1 to 5 are supplied in Macmillan's Sets of Mathematical Instruments. The Elementary Set, on card, 3d. net. In Metal Pocket Case: The School Set, 1s. net; The Beginner's Set, 1s. 6d. net; The Junior Set, 2s. net; The Senior Set, 2s. 6d. net.

6. Tracing paper. Squared paper.

It is also very desirable that pupils should have an opportunity of seeing and handling Models of the simpler Solid Figures.

A set of Models for use with this book has been specially prepared, and may be obtained (price 6s., in box, including carriage to any part of the United Kingdom) direct from the manufacturer

G. CUSSONS
The Technical Works
Lower Broughton
MANCHESTER

CHAPTER I

SOLIDS, SURFACES, LINES

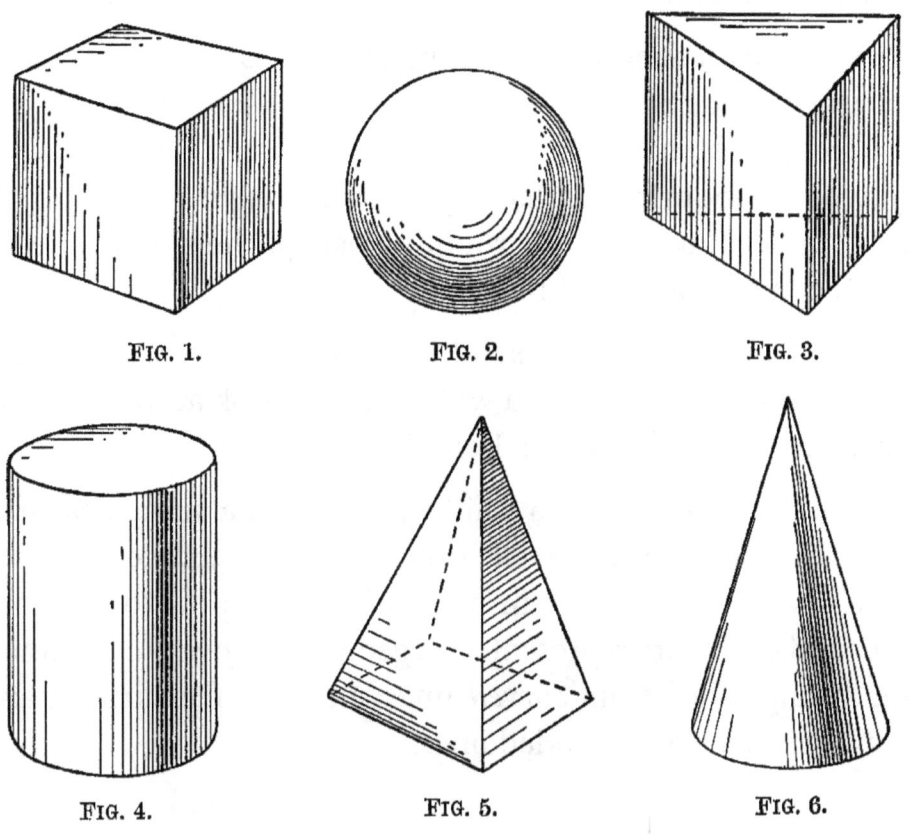

FIG. 1.   FIG. 2.   FIG. 3.

FIG. 4.   FIG. 5.   FIG. 6.

We have here some wooden models of what are called **solids** or **solid figures,** and they are differently named according to their shapes. That, for instance, of which a drawing is given in Figure 1, is called a **cube;** that shown in Figure 2 is a **sphere;** that in Figure 4 is a **cylinder;** and that in Figure 5 is a **pyramid.**

The *outside* of these solid models, the part which we see and touch, is called the **surface**.

Sometimes the surface of a solid is all in one piece, as in the sphere (Figure 2). Sometimes it consists of several parts: for instance in the cube (Figure 1) the surface consists of six parts, all flat; these are called **faces.** Again, in the cylinder (Figure 4) the surface consists of *three* parts, one rounded and the other two flat. Once more, the surface of the cone (Figure 6) is in *two* parts, one rounded and running to a point, the other flat.

Let us now see how two neighbouring parts of a surface meet. They meet in **edges** or **lines;** and these lines are sometimes *straight,* and sometimes *curved.* In the prism and pyramid (Figures 3 and 5) two neighbouring flat faces meet in a *straight* line; while in the cylinder (Figure 4) the rounded part of the surface meets each flat end in a *curved* line.

How do the *edges* of a solid meet? If two edges meet at all, they meet at a **point**; as you will see if you look at the edges of a cube or pyramid (Figures 1 and 5).

You now know what a solid is, and what a surface is; and you have learned that surfaces, or parts of a surface, meet in lines and that lines meet in points. We have now to see how lines and points are represented in geometry; how *straight* lines are distinguished from *curved* lines; and how flat surfaces are distinguished from rounded ones.

Points. The smallest dot you can make on your paper with a sharp pencil, or with a fine needle, will give you an idea of what is meant by a geometrical point. A point is so minute that we do not think of its length, breadth, size, or shape: all we have to consider is its *position*.

SOLIDS, SURFACES, LINES

As we have seen, a point marks the place where two lines cross one another. Points are named and distinguished from one another by attaching letters to them: thus we speak of the point **A**, or the point **B**.

•A

ˣ
B̥

Lines. We represent a line by drawing the point of a sharp pencil over a surface, such as a sheet of paper: this shows that *a line is traced out by a moving point*.

Several kinds of line are shown in the margin.

All lines have *length,* some more, some less; but the *breadth* of a well drawn line is so small that no notice is taken of it in geometrical work: indeed, the finer your pencil-trace, the better it represents a line.

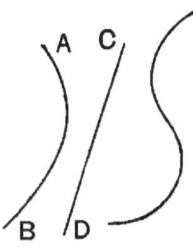

What we have to consider in a line is its *length* and *position*, and whether it is *straight* or *curved*. A line is named by two letters: thus we speak of the line **AB**, or the line **CD**.

Straight lines. No doubt you already know the meaning of the word *straight* well enough to give examples of straight lines. A very fine thread tightly stretched is a good instance of a straight line; so are the edges of the set squares which you are to use as rulers. But *straightness* needs some further illustration.

(i) When you walk along a winding lane you notice that your direction is continually changing; and if, for instance, you faced North when you started, you may presently find yourself facing East. But when you walk along a *straight* road, there is no change of direction as you

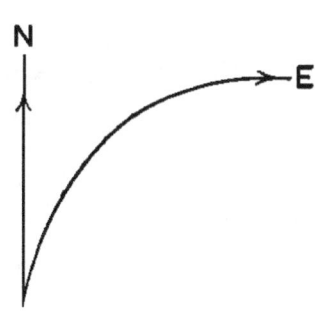

advance; and if you faced North at starting, you will continue to face North.

(ii) In a field there are two trees whose positions are marked by the letters **A** and **B**. Suppose you wish to go from one tree to 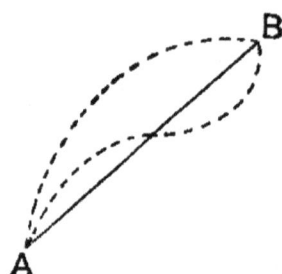 the other by the *shortest* way. You can see at once what course you must steer. You must go *straight* from **A** to **B**. There are numberless *curved* lines along which you could go from one tree to the other, but the shortest way of all is the *straight* line. You notice that we have said *the* straight line; for you can see for yourself that there can only be *one straight* line leading from **A** to **B**.

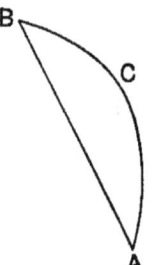 (iii) A strip of ground has been enclosed by two fences. One of these, **AB**, is straight: can the other be straight also? Clearly not; for we have already seen that there cannot be more than one *straight* line between **A** and **B**, though many curved lines such as **ACB**.

(iv) We will draw a curved line, and call it **AB**; then we will rule a straight line **CD** across it. You see that you can place your ruler so that the straight line will cut the curved one at *two* points, perhaps even more than two. Now take a *straight* line **AB**, and rule another straight line **CD** across it. Can you now place your ruler so as to cut **AB** in more than one point? You will soon find that you cannot.

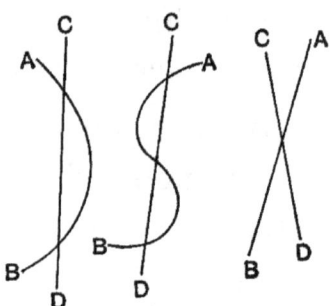

SOLIDS, SURFACES, LINES

Let us now put together what we have learned about straight lines.

(i) *A straight line has the same direction throughout its length.*

(ii) *The straight line which joins two points is the shortest distance between them; and there is only one such straight line.*

(iii) *Two straight lines cannot enclose a space.*

(iv) *If two straight lines cross one another they can only cut at one point.*

When you rule a straight line between two points **A** and **B**, you are said to **join AB**.

Test of straightness. We can find if a given line **AB** is straight or not by means of a copy of it made on tracing-paper. If by turning the tracing either *round* or *over* we can in any way make the given line and the tracing enclose a space, then the given line is not straight. But if in *all* such positions the tracing can be made to fit exactly over the given line throughout its whole length, then we may conclude that the latter is straight. Apply this test to the two lines drawn below.

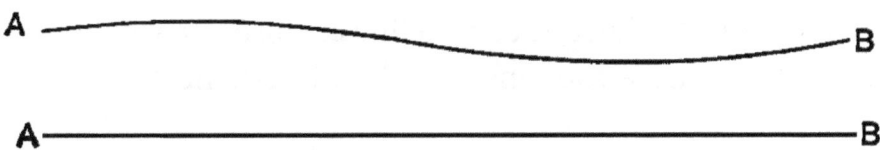

Planes. Several different kinds of surfaces have been shown to you, and you have noticed that some are rounded or curved, and some are **plane,** that is to say, *flat.* How can we tell a plane surface from a curved one?

Lay the straight-edge of a ruler on a table, and notice that the *whole length* of the edge always rests upon the surface, *in whatever position the ruler is placed*. But if the ruler is placed in the hollow of a basin, only the ends rest on the surface: or again, if the straight-edge is laid against a sphere, it touches the surface at one point only.

Thus *a surface is* **plane** *when the straight line joining* **any** *two points on it lies entirely on the surface.*

NOTE. There are some curved surfaces, such as those of a *cylinder* and *cone,* along which a ruler will lie in *certain directions,* but not in *all* directions. The teacher should illustrate this with his models.

Exercise 1. What is the least number of *straight* lines that can enclose a space?

Rule *three* straight lines so as to enclose a space.

Rule *four* straight lines so as to enclose a space.

Exercise 2. Can two *curved* lines enclose a space? If so, make a drawing either free-hand or with compasses, showing a space enclosed by two curved lines.

Exercise 3. Can *one* curved line enclose a space? Make a drawing to illustrate your answer, either free-hand or with your compasses.

Exercise 4. Mark a point on your paper, and call it **A**. How many straight lines, having different directions, can be drawn through the point **A**?

Rule *five* straight lines passing through **A**.

SOLIDS, SURFACES, LINES

Exercise 5. Mark two points **A** and **B**. *Join* **AB**. Observe that the position of a *straight* line is fixed if we know *two* points through which it passes. How many *curved* lines can be drawn from **A** to **B**? Draw *three* such lines, either free-hand or with your compasses.

Exercise 6. Mark *three* points **A**, **B**, and **C**, placing them so that they do not lie all in a straight line. How many straight lines can be drawn by joining these points in pairs? Draw all these lines.

Exercise 7. Repeat Exercise 6, but take *four* points **A**, **B**, **C**, and **D**, no three of which lie in a straight line, and join them in pairs.

CHAPTER II

MEASUREMENT OF STRAIGHT LINES

In practical geometry you will frequently have to measure the lengths of the lines you draw. For this purpose you have a scale which shows inches along one of its edges, each inch being divided into 10 equal parts: along another edge *centimetres* are marked, and each centimetre is also divided into 10 equal parts or *millimetres*.

Begin by carefully noticing the length of 1 inch and of 1 centimetre, so that you may be able to guess pretty nearly (even without measurement) how many inches or how many centimetres there are in a given line.

In writing down your measurements use the following abbreviations:

in. for *inch*; *cm.* for *centimetre*; *mm.* for *millimetre*.

Inches may also be denoted by the mark ("). Thus 3" means 3 *inches*.

The units on your scale are divided into *tenths* in order that your measurements may be recorded *decimally*: Thus

(i) *Three and seven-tenths inches* should be written 3.7 in., or 3.7".

(ii) *Eight-tenths of an inch* should be written 0.8 in., or 0.8"

(iii) *Five centimetres four millimetres* should be written 5.4 cm.

MEASUREMENT OF STRAIGHT LINES

Exercise 1. Measure the lengths of **AB** and **CD** in inches and tenths of an inch.

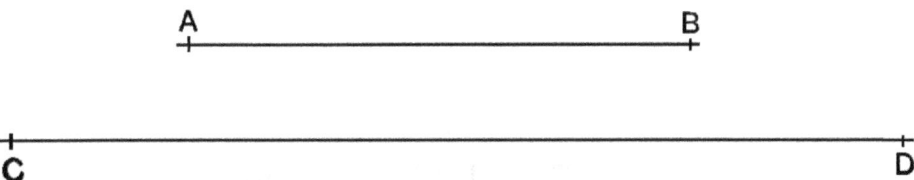

Exercise 2. Measure the above lines **AB** and **CD** as nearly as you can in centimetres and millimetres.

Exercise 3. Measure **AX** and **XB** in inches and tenths of an inch, and add your results together. Test your work by measuring **AB**.

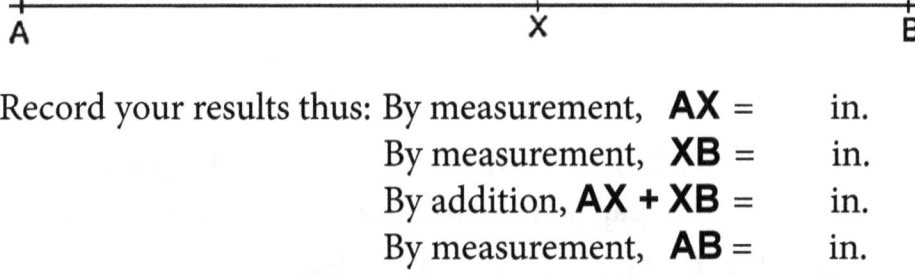

Record your results thus: By measurement, **AX** =   in.
By measurement, **XB** =   in.
By addition, **AX + XB** =   in.
By measurement, **AB** =   in.

Exercise 4. Measure **AX** and **XB** in centimetres and millimetres, and find their difference. Test your result by measuring **AB**.

Record your results as above.

Exercise 5. (i) Measure **AB**, **AX**, and **XY** in inches and tenths of an inch: hence reckon the length of **YB**, and test your result by measurement.

(ii) Measure **AY**, **YB**, and **XB** in centimetres, and hence find **AY** + **YB** − **XB**. What line should you now measure to test your result?

In each case arrange your results in tabular form.

Exercise 6. Draw straight lines to show the following lengths:

    2.6 in.,   5.0 cm.,   1.8″,   4.7 cm.,   0.8 in.
    8.2 cm.,   3.1″,   0.7 cm.,   9 mm.,   33 mm.

(Subdivision of a line by measurement)

Exercise 7. How would you find the middle point in the length of a strip of paper (i) by folding, (ii) by measurement?

Exercise 8. Draw a line **AB** of length 3″. What is the length of half **AB**? From **AB** mark off one-half, and thus find **O** the middle point of **AB**. Test your work by measuring **OB**.

A straight line is said to be **bisected** when it is divided into *two equal* parts.

Exercise 9. Draw a line **AB** of length 8.1 cm. What is the length of one-third of **AB**? With your dividers step off along **AB** one-third of its length, and thus divide **AB** into three equal parts.

A straight line is said to be **trisected** when it is divided into *three* equal parts.

MEASUREMENT OF STRAIGHT LINES

Exercise 10. Draw a line **AB** of length 7.2 cm. By measurement, as explained above, cut off from it **AP** equal to *half* **AB**, and **AQ** equal to *one-third* **AB**. Find with your dividers how many times **PQ** is contained in **AB**. Explain your result by finding the value of ½ − ⅓.

(Comparison of 1 inch with 1 centimetre)

Exercise 11. Take 1 inch in your dividers, and apply them to your centimetre scale. How many centimetres and millimetres do you find in 1 inch?

It is impossible even with the greatest care to measure a length with perfect correctness; but the error is likely to be smaller *in proportion* in measuring a longer than in measuring a shorter length.

Exercise 12. Find the length of 1 inch in centimetres by measuring a length of 4 inches, and then dividing the result by 4.

Thus 4 inches =   cm.
∴ 1 inch =   cm.

Exercise 13. Measure a length of 1 centimetre against your inch scale. Then measure a length of 10 centimetres, and divide the result by 10. Compare the two equivalents of 1 cm., and observe that the second is likely to be the more correct.

(Distances represented by Lines drawn to Scale)

A map or plan is a small but exact flat copy of the country or ground it represents. Therefore by measuring on a map the distance between two dots which mark certain towns, we may reckon the real distance between the towns themselves, provided we know the *scale* on which the map is drawn. For instance, if 1 inch measured on the map stands for 10 miles, then 2″ stands for 20 miles; 4.5″ for 45 miles; and so on. Such a map is said to be drawn on *the scale of* 10 *miles to* 1 *inch*.

Exercise 14. The plan of an estate is drawn on the scale of 75 yards to 1 inch:

(i) What distance on the ground is represented by 3.6″ on the map?

$$\text{Here 1 inch represents 75 yards;}$$
$$\therefore \ 3.6 \text{ inches} \ldots\ldots\ldots 75 \text{ yards} \times 3.6$$
$$= 270 \text{ yards.}$$

(ii) What length on the map will represent 405 yards?

$$\text{Here 75 yards are represented by 1 inch;}$$
$$\therefore \ 405 \text{ yards} \ldots\ldots\ldots\ldots 1 \text{ inch} \times {}^{405}/_{75}$$
$$= 5.4''.$$

Exercise 15. A plan is drawn on the scale of 100 metres to 1 centimetre:

(i) What actual distances are represented on the map by 4.0 cm., by 5.6 cm., by 0.8 cm.?

(ii) Draw lines to represent 450 metres, 720 metres, 580 metres, and 60 metres.

Exercise 16. On a map in which 1″ stands for 20 miles, the distance between Halifax and Hull is represented by 3.2″. What is the actual distance?

Bedford is 86 miles from Norwich: how far apart would they be on the map?

Exercise 17. The points marked **Sa.**, **So.**, **W** represent the positions of Salisbury, Southampton, and Winchester on a map whose scale is 10 miles to 1 inch.

Find by measurement and reckoning the actual distances between Salisbury and Winchester, Winchester and Southampton, Southampton and Salisbury.

MEASUREMENT OF STRAIGHT LINES

×
S*a*.

×
W

×
S*o*.

[In the following Exercises plans are to be drawn on squared paper ruled to tenths of an inch, and the results are to be got by measurement and reckoning.]

Exercise 18. I walk 4 miles due North, then 3 miles due East. Draw a plan to show my journey, making 1 in. stand for 1 mile; then by measurement find how far I am from my starting point.

Exercise 19. Draw the ground-plan of a room, 30 feet long by 20 feet wide, making 1″ represent 10 feet. Find as nearly as you can the actual distance between two opposite corners.

Exercise 20. An upright pole, standing 25 feet high, is stayed by a rope carried from the top to a point on the ground 15 feet from the foot of the pole. Represent this by a drawing (scale 10 feet to 1 inch); and find the length of the rope.

Exercise 21. A ladder reaches a window-sill 15 feet high, and the foot of the ladder rests on the ground 8 feet from the front of the house. Draw a plan (scale 5 feet to 1 inch), and use it to find the length of the ladder.

Exercise 22. Looking Eastward from my house, I see a church tower which I know to be 2 miles distant. Looking North I see a second tower 1½ miles away. Draw a plan (scale 1 mile to 1 inch), and find how far the towers are apart.

Exercise 23. A ship on leaving harbour sails 22 miles South, then again 22 miles West. Represent her course on the scale of 10 miles to 1 inch, and find her distance from the harbour.

Exercise 24. In rowing across a river 48 metres wide, a man was carried 16 metres down stream. Represent this on a plan (scale 20 metres to 1 inch); hence find the distance between the starting point and landing-point.

CHAPTER III

STRAIGHT LINES CONTINUED

⁎⁎ *This Section may be postponed for revision.*

If you measure the same line in several ways, some of your results may be a little too large and some a little too small. The *average* of your results is likely to be nearer the truth than any single result. To find the average, add your results together, and divide their sum by the number of them.

Exercise 1. Measure **AB** in inches and also in centimetres; and hence express 1 inch in terms of cm. and mm.

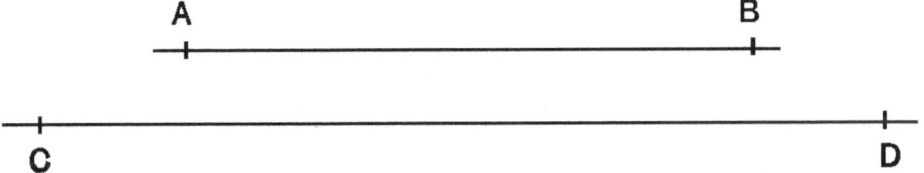

Measure **CD**, and repeat the process. Now find the average of your two results.

(Judging Lengths, Errors, Relative Errors)

It is important that you should train your eye to subdivide any unit of length into *tenths* without actual measurement. Remember that *one-half* = *five*-tenths: this gives a standard to judge by. Fix your eye on the middle point, and mentally divide each half into five equal parts.

Exercise 2. The lines marked **AB** are all 1 inch long. State in each case how many tenths of an inch there are in **AP**; then verify your answer by measurement.

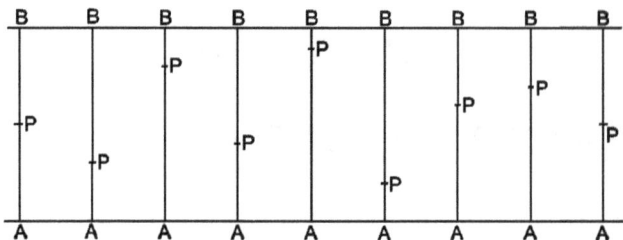

Exercise 3. Draw six lines each 1 inch long, calling one end **A**. Then mark a point **P** in each (without measurement) so that, as nearly as you can judge, **AP** may be in succession 0.4″, 0.7″, 0.2″, 0.9″, 0.3″, 0.6″.

Check your attempts by measurement.

Exercise 4. (i) Judge as nearly as you can in inches and centimetres the lengths of the lines given below.

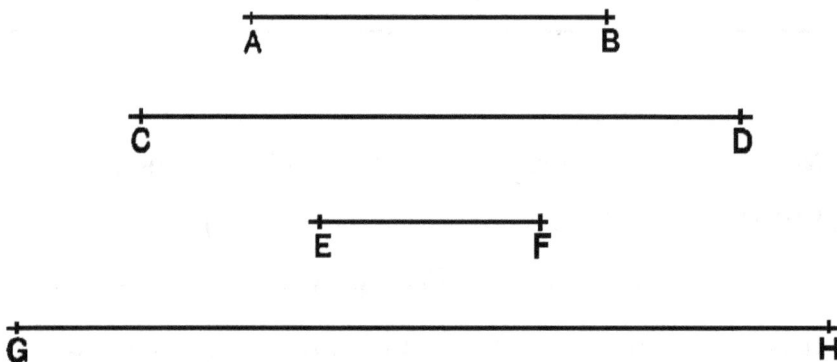

Check your estimates by measurement, and tabulate the results as on the next page, leaving the last column blank for the present.

STRAIGHT LINES CONTINUED

	Measured length.	Estimated length.	Actual error.	Percentage error.
AB	in.	in.	in.	
	cm.	cm.	cm.	

₊ *Other lines of greater length and not all horizontal should be given by the teacher.*

(ii) Draw lines as nearly as you can judge without measuring to show 6 cm., 2.0″, 8 cm., 3.5″. Measure your attempts; note your errors, and tabulate the results.

In judging the importance of an error we do not care so much whether it is large or small, as whether it amounts to a large or small fraction of the quantity we are estimating. For instance: suppose that in guessing the length of a line whose real length is 5 cm. we are wrong by 1 cm.; while in guessing a line 20 cm. long we are wrong by 2 cm. The actual error in the latter case is greater than in the former, but it is really of less importance. For in the second case the error is only *one-tenth* of the real length, that is, *one in ten*; while in the first case it is *one-fifth*, or *one in five*. Errors thus measured as fractions of the true value are called **relative errors**: and it is convenient to reduce them to a fixed standard, as so many *in one-hundred*, or so many *per cent*. Take the following case:

Real length.	Estimated length.	Actual error.	Percentage error.
8.0 cm.	7.5 cm.	0.5 cm.	

Here on a real length of 8 cm. the error is 0.5 cm.

∴ .... 100 cm. the error is $0.5 \text{ cm.} \times {}^{100}/_{8}$

$= 6¼$ cm.

That is, the error is at the rate of *6¼ in one hundred,* or *6¼ per cent.* We may now enter 6¼ in the last column.

Exercise 5. Fill up the percentage column in Exercise 4, giving the percentage correct to one decimal figure.

Hitherto the lines which you have had to measure in inches and tenths of an inch have contained an exact number of tenths. This will not always be so. For example

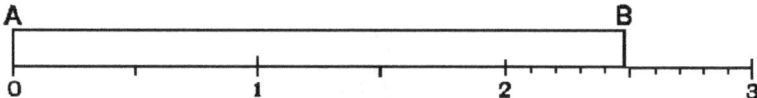

the line **AB** above (where ruler is enlarged) represents a line that is more than 2.4″ and less than 2.5″. In this case we may mentally divide the tenth in which **B** falls into *ten* equal parts, that is to say, into *hundredths of an inch,* and judge as nearly as we can how many of these hundredths are to be added to 2.4. In this instance about *seven*-hundredths should be added, so that the length of **AB** is nearly 2.47″.

Exercise 6. Draw on squared paper a figure like that below, making **OA** and **OB** each 2″ long. Put **P, Q, R** and **X, Y, Z** at the half-inch divisions; then measure **AB, RZ, QY, PX** as nearly as you can in *inches, tenths* and *hundredths.*

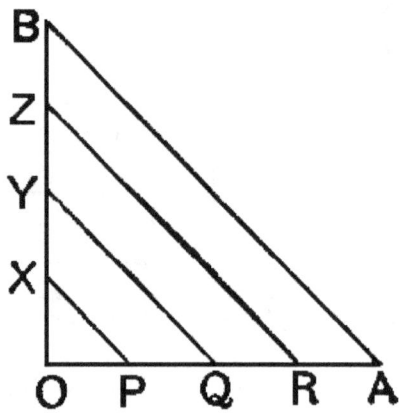

CHAPTER IV

CIRCLES

Mark a point **O** on your paper. Take a distance of 5 cm. between the points of your compasses; then, placing the steel point at **O**, turn the compasses between your fore-finger and thumb so as to draw a curved line with the pencil-point.

As the curved line is being traced out, notice carefully that the pencil-point always keeps the same distance from **O**. What distance? Notice also that the pencil returns to its starting point, so as to close the curve. Why is this?

The curve you have thus drawn is called a **circle,** and the point **O** is its **centre.** Sometimes the word *circle* means the space enclosed by the curve, and then the curve itself is said to be the **circumference** of the circle.

Exercise 1. Mark a few points, say four, anywhere on the circumference of the circle you have drawn: call them **A, B, C, D**. Join **OA, OB, OC, OD**. How do you know that these lines are all equal! Tell their length without measuring them.

Straight lines drawn from the centre of a circle to its circumference are called **radii.** All the radii of a circle are equal.

Exercise 2. Mark a fixed point **O** on your paper: then with your compasses mark any *four* points whose distance from **O** is 2.0". How many points could you mark whose distance from **O** is 2.0"? Draw a curve to pass through all of them.

Exercise 3. Suppose a point **X** is taken 1.7" from the centre of the circle you have just drawn (Exercise 2); another point **Y** is 2.0", and a third point **Z** is 2.3" from the centre. Which of these points is on the circumference? Which outside it? Which within it?

Exercise 4. Invent some other means, besides compasses, by which a circle could be drawn having a fixed point **O** as centre.

Exercise 5. Now explain in your own words what a circle is, telling how the circumference is related to the centre.

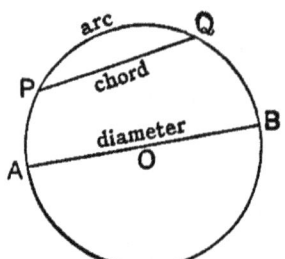

Taking a point **O** as centre, draw a circle with a radius of 1.5". Then through the centre **O** draw any straight line ended each way by the circumference. Such a line is called a **diameter,** and is represented in the Figure by **AB**.

Exercise 6. What is the length of **AB** in your drawing? Answer this without measuring. Are all diameters of a circle equal?

Now carefully cut your circle out, and fold it about the diameter **AB**, thus dividing the circle into two parts. Do you find that one part fits exactly over the other? If so, this shows that the two parts *are of the same size and shape.* Flatten out the circle; rule any other diameter, and fold the circle about it as before. Again you find that one part fits exactly over the other. All this we express by saying that a circle is **symmetrical** about any diameter.

The two equal parts into which a circle is divided by a diameter are called **semi-circles.**

An **arc** (i.e. *bow*) is any part of the circumference of a circle,

A **chord** (i.e. *string*) is the straight line joining the ends of an arc.

CIRCLES

Exercise 7. Draw a circle of diameter 3.0″, and on the circumference mark a point **X**. From **X** draw two chords, one 1.5″ long, the other 2.0″ long. What is the length of the longest chord in this circle?

Exercise 8. In the Figure on the opposing page notice that the chord **PQ** divides the circumference into *two* arcs. Point them out. Can a chord ever cut off two *equal* arcs? Which is the longer line, an arc, or the chord which joins its ends?

(Two or more circles, Intersection of circles)

Exercise 9. Mark a point **O** on your paper, and from **O** as centre draw three circles, one of radius 3.5 cm., the next of radius 4.0 cm., the third of radius 4.5 cm. Notice that the circumferences do not cross or cut one another. Why not?

Circles which have the same centre are said to be **concentric**.

Exercise 10. (i) Take two points **A** and **B**, 7 cm. apart. With **A** as centre draw a circle of radius 4 cm.; and with **B** as centre draw a circle of radius 2 cm. Explain why each circle is outside the other. What is the shortest distance between the circumferences?

(ii) Again take two points **A** and **B**, 7 cm. apart; and, as before, with **A** as centre draw a circle of radius 4 cm. But this time draw from centre **B** a circle of radius 5 cm. Why do these circles overlap? At how many points do the circumferences cut one another?

(iii) Once more take two points **A** and **B**, 7 cm. apart, and with **A** and **B** as centres draw two circles, one of radius 4 cm., the other of radius 3 cm. Do the circumferences cross one another? Do they meet? If your work is carefully done, the two circles just *touch* one another. Where is the touching point? Say why.

Exercise 11. Take two points **A** and **B**, 2 cm. apart; and with centre **A** draw a circle of radius 5 cm. With centre **B** draw a circle of radius 3 cm. How does this circle meet the first, and where is the meeting-point?

Exercise 12. Can you draw two circles which cut one another at more than two points? Try.

Exercise 13. Take two points 3″ apart, and call them **A** and **B**. With centre **A** and radius 2½″ draw a circle. With centre **B** and radius 2″ draw a second circle. Call the points at which the circles cut one another **P** and **Q**. How far is **P** from **A** and from **B**? How far is **Q** from **A** and from **B**?

Exercise 14. Take two points **A** and **B**, 8 cm. apart. Find with your compasses a point which is 6 cm. from **A** and also 6 cm. from **B**. Can you find more than one such point? How many?

Exercise 15. Draw a line 2.5″ long, and find with your compasses a point that is 2.0″ from each end. How many such points are there?

Exercise 16. Take two points **X** and **Y**, 9 cm. apart. Find a point which is 6 cm. from **X** and 5 cm. from **Y**. How many such points are there?

Exercise 17. Draw a line 3.3″ long, and find two points each of which is 2.2″ from one end and 1.8″ from the other.

Exercise 18. Two forts defending the mouth of a river, one on each side, are 10 kilometres apart: their guns have an effective range of 6000 metres. Draw a plan (scale 1 km. to 1 cm.) showing what part of the river is exposed to fire from both forts.

CIRCLES

PROBLEM 1

To bisect a straight line **AB** *with ruler and compasses.*

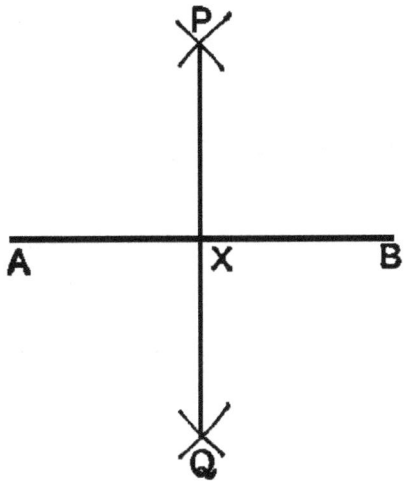

[The given straight line **AB** may be of any length: about 3″ to 4″ will be convenient, but do not measure it.]

Construction. Take in your compasses any length that appears to you to be greater than half **AB** (say about 2½″); and then with centre **A** draw arcs on each side of **AB**.

Again with centre **B**, and with the *same radius* as before, draw arcs to cut the first arcs as shown in the Figure. Call the cutting points **P** and **Q**.

Join **PQ**, and put **X** at the point where this line crosses **AB**.

Now take **AX** in your dividers, and see if **BX** is equal to it.

(Further Tests)

(i) Mark the points **A**, **B**, and **X** on tracing-paper, and turning it round, place the trace of **A** on **B**, and the trace of **B** on **A**. Where does the trace of **X** fall? How does this experiment show that **AB** has been bisected at **X**?

(ii) If the arcs drawn from centre **B** had a greater radius than those drawn from centre **A**, would **X** still be the middle point of **AB**? If not, towards which end of **AB** would **X** lie? Take your compasses and try. You see then that **X** is the middle point of **AB** *because we have worked from centre* **B** *in exactly the same way as from centre* **A**.

(iii) Why did we take a radius *greater* than half **AB**? What would have happened if the radius had been *less* than half **AB**? or exactly half **AB**? Take your compasses and try.

Exercise 19. Draw a line 8.5 cm. long, and bisect it with ruler and compasses. Test your drawing with the dividers.

Exercise 20. Draw a line 3.4″ long. Find the middle point **X** *by measurement*. Now bisect **AB** *by construction,* and see if the line **PQ** passes through **X**.

Exercise 21. Draw a line 9.6 cm. long. Bisect it by construction; then bisect each half.

Draw a circle, say of radius 2.0″, and with *the same radius* mark off points round the circumference. How many steps can you thus take? **Six** exactly. Are the *arcs* which you thus cut off each 2″ in length? Are they more or less than 2″? Join the points of division in order. Are the *chords* each 2″ in length? Why so? Join the centre to each point of division, and thus complete the pattern shown in the margin.

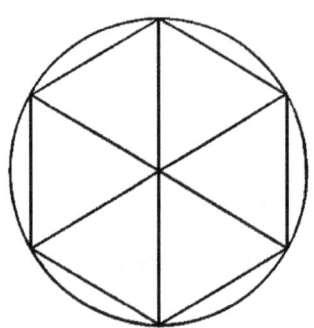

Exercise 22. Invent some simple experiment, for instance by cutting out, or folding, or by means of a tracing, to show that the six arcs are of equal length (though not 2″). Try to find the length of one of these arcs by laying a thread along it, straightening the thread out before measurement.

CIRCLES

Exercise 23. Draw the patterns of which small copies are given below. Your drawings should be twice the size of the copies.

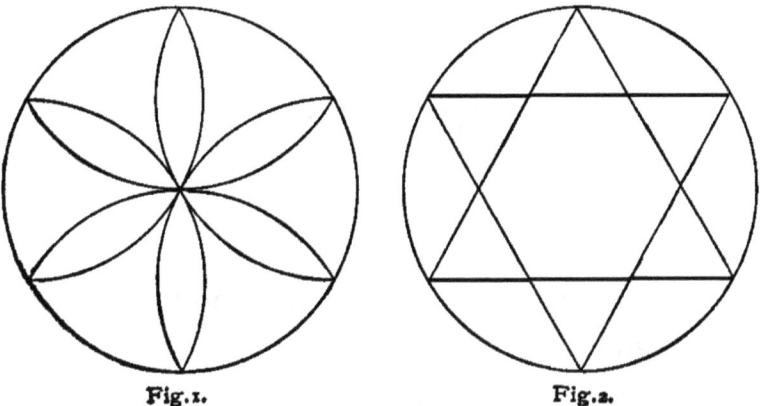

Fig. 1. Fig. 2.

CHAPTER V

ANGLES

Any two straight lines drawn from a point **O** form what is called an **Angle**.

The point **O** is the **vertex**, and the lines are the **arms** of the angle.

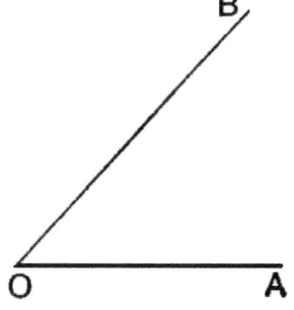

Put **A** at any point on one arm, and **B** at any point on the other; then the angle at **O** is named either by the letters **AOB** or by **BOA**, the letter **O** at the vertex being between the other two.

The sign "∠" is used for the word *angle*.

Thus the angle in the Figure is called the ∠ **AOB** or the ∠ **BOA**.

Exercise 1. Draw two straight lines forming an angle at the point **O**. Put **A** and **P** at any two points in one arm, and **B** and **Q** at any two points in the other arm. Then name the angle at **O** by three letters in all the ways you can.

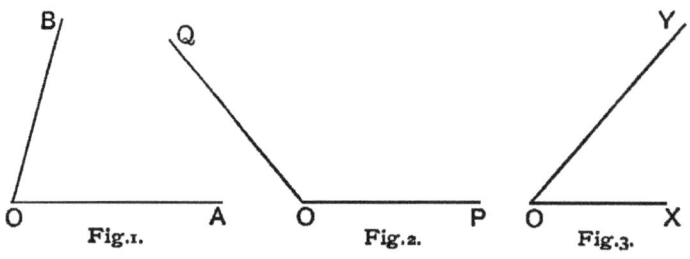

Figures 1, 2, and 3 represent three angles. In Figure 2 you see that the arms are *more widely opened out* than in Figure 1; while in Figure 3 the arms are *less widely opened out* than in Figure 1. This we express by saying that

> the angle **POQ** is *greater than* the angle **AOB**;

> the angle **XOY** is *less than* the angle **AOB**.

Thus the size of an angle does not depend on the length of its arms, but only on the *slope* or *inclination* of one arm to the other.

How can we find out whether the angle **ABC** is *equal* to the angle **XYZ**? Here is one way.

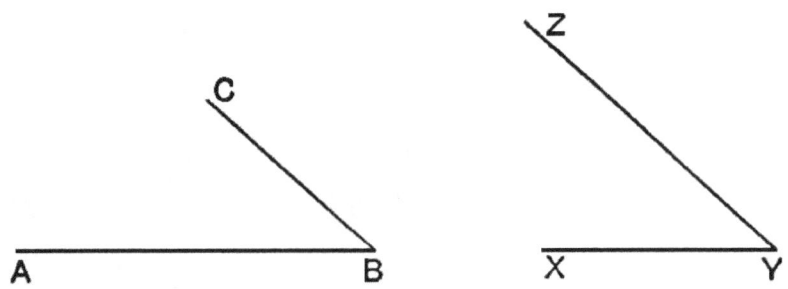

Copy the angle **ABC** on tracing-paper. Move the tracing so that the vertex **B** comes over the vertex **Y**; then place the trace of **BA** *along* **YX**. This you can always do whether the two angles are equal or not. Now observe where the trace of **BC** falls. Does it lie *along* **YZ**? If so, the angles **ABC**, **XYZ** are equal, though their arms are not of the same length.

What conclusion would you have drawn if **BC** had fallen *within* the angle **XYZ**? Or again, if **BC** had fallen outside the angle **XYZ**?

Exercise 2. Draw two angles making them equal to one another as nearly as you can judge, but do not make the arms of the same length. Try with tracing-paper if the two angles are really equal; and if not, say which is the greater.

Exercise 3. Draw two angles, one greater than the other. Give the larger angle shorter arms than the smaller one.

Take your compasses, and holding one leg fixed along the desk, open them gradually out. Observe that you make the other leg *rotate about the pivot* like the hand of a watch, and that as you do so, you constantly increase the angle between the legs.

We may thus suppose an angle **AOB** to be formed by a *fixed* line **OA** and a *rotating* line **OB**, the size of the angle **AOB** being given by the *amount of turning* required to bring the rotating arm from its first position **OA** to its subsequent position **OB**.

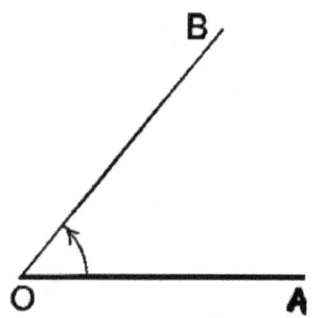

Exercise 4. When two straight lines **OA**, **OB** meet at a point **O**, *two* angles are formed. The first is got by supposing **OB** to have moved from **OA** into its present position by turning the *shorter way round*, marked (i); the other by supposing **OB** to have turned the *longer way round*, marked (ii). The latter angle is said to be **reflex**. Illustrate this by drawing any angle; then place one end of a penholder at the vertex, and turn it from one arm to the other in opposite ways. Which way gives the reflex angle?

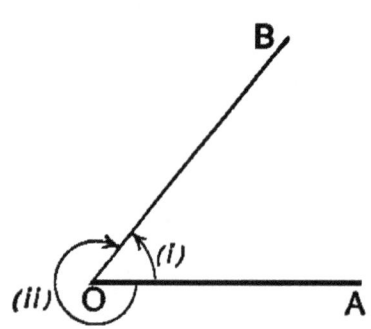

Unless the word *reflex* is specially used, *the angle at* **O** will always mean the smaller of the two angles formed by the arms.

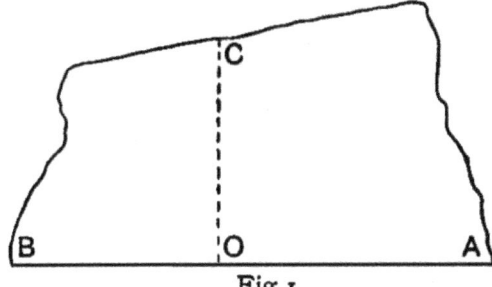
Fig. 1.

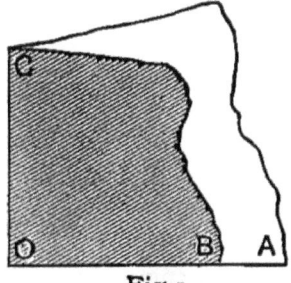
Fig. 2.

Take a piece of paper having a straight edge **AB** (Figure 1). Fold, as in Figure 2, so as to bring the point **B** over on to the straight edge towards **A**. Open out the paper, and mark the crease **OC**. The angles **AOC**, **BOC** are equal. Why so?

Try the experiment two or three times, and fit together the folded papers. Do you find that all the angles you get in this way are of the same size?

In each case you have a straight line **OC** meeting a straight line **AB** in such a way that the angles made on either side of **OC** are equal. Such angles are called **right-angles**; and our experiments show that all right angles are equal. Thus a right angle may be taken as a standard with which to compare other angles.

OC is said to be **at right angles** to **AB**; or **perpendicular** to **AB**.

A right angle is divided into 90 equal parts called degrees (°).

That is, *one right angle = 90°*.

An **acute** angle is less than one right angle.

An **obtuse** angle is greater than one right angle.

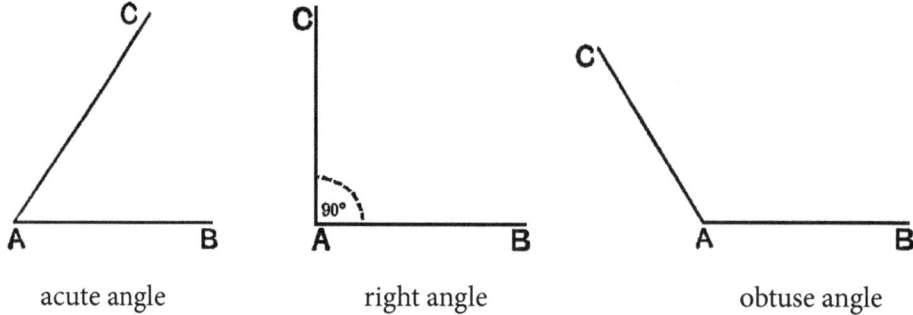

acute angle   right angle   obtuse angle

Exercise 5. Fold a piece of paper of any shape, and call the straight folded edge **AB**. Then (without opening the paper out) fold again so as to bring **B** over **A**. On unfolding, the creases cross one another, forming four angles. What can you tell of these angles? Are they equal? Are they right angles? Say why.

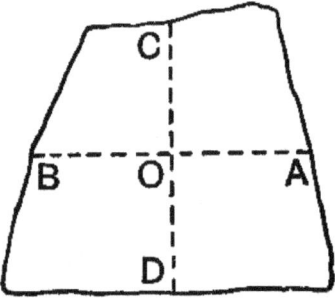

Exercise 6. A line, starting from the position **OA**, rotates about **O**; and having made *a complete revolution*, returns to **OA**. Through how many degrees has it revolved?

Through how many degrees does the line revolve in making *one quarter* of a revolution? In making *one half* a revolution?

Observe that

    a **complete** revolution corresponds to **4** right angles.

    a **quarter** revolution   .... 1 right angle.

    a **half** revolution   .... 2 right angles.

Exercise 7. Through how many degrees does the minute-hand of a clock revolve in ¼ hour, in ½ hour, in ¾ hour, in 1 hour?

ANGLES

Exercise 8. Through how many degrees does the minute-hand revolve in 5 minutes, in 25 minutes, in 36 minutes? How long will it take to turn through 48°? Through 102°? Through 9°?

Exercise 9. If a wheel makes 10 revolutions a minute, through how many degrees will it turn in 1 second?

(Angles at the Centre of a Circle)

Exercise 10. In the marginal figure the angles **AOD, DOC, COE, EOB** have been made all equal. How many degrees are there in the ∠ **AOD**? In the ∠ **AOC**? In the ∠ **AOE**? In the ∠ **AOB**?

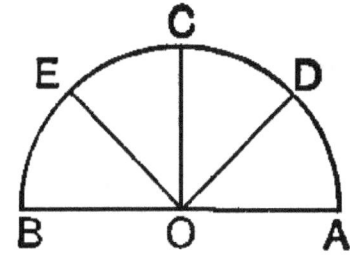

The angle **AOB** is called a **straight** angle.

Draw a semi-circle, radius 2″; cut it out, and obtain the lines **OC, OD, OE** by folding.

The figure formed by the radii **OA, OC** and the arc **AC** is called **a quadrant**, or quarter, of a circle. Point out another quadrant.

Exercise 11. In the marginal figure the angles **AOP, POQ**, etc., have been made all equal. How many degrees are there in each of the ∠ˢ **AOP, AOQ, AOC, AOR, AOS, AOB**? How many degrees in the ∠ˢ **SOC, ROP**?

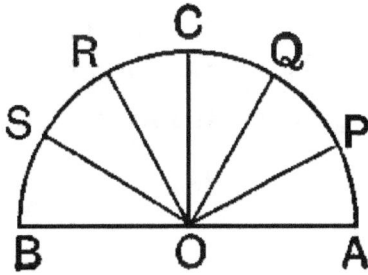

Exercise 12. Draw a circle of radius 5 cm. Take *any* distance you like in your compasses, and with this distance mark off points round the circumference. Call the points **A**, **B**, **C**, etc., and join them to the centre **O**. Now, what are the equal lengths you have been stepping off? Certainly equal *chords*, though you have not actually drawn them.

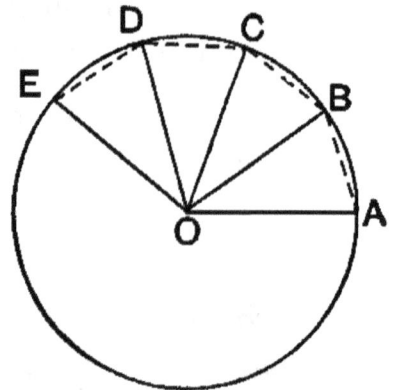

Try to invent some practical way (either by means of tracing, or by cutting out and fitting one part over the other) of finding if in measuring off equal *chords* you have also cut off equal *arcs*. Are the *angles* **AOB**, **BOC**, **COD**, etc. equal too?

Exercise 13. In the Figure of the last Exercise, how many times does the arc **EA** contain the arc **BA**? How many times does the ∠ **EOA** contain the ∠ **BOA**?

Thus in a circle (or in *equal* circles) you have found by experiment that when you measure off equal *chords*, you thereby cut off equal *arcs*; and by cutting off equal arcs, you can make equal *angles* at the centre. This principle is most important, and is used again and again in practical geometry.

ANGLES

(Use of the Protractor)

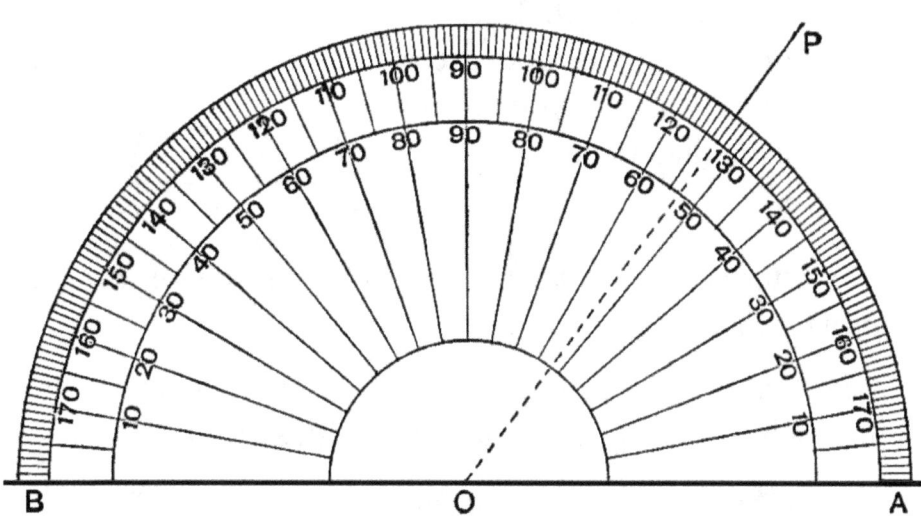

Your protractor shows a semi-circular arc divided into 180 equal parts, which for convenience are numbered from each end.

(i) *To measure the number of degrees in a given angle*, place the protractor with its centre at the vertex, and the diameter in line with one of the arms of the angle; then observe the mark of division on the rim under which the other arm passes.

(ii) *To make an angle of a given number of degrees* (say 53°), draw one arm **OA**; place the protractor with its centre on **O** and its diameter in line with **OA**; mark a point on your paper as close as you can to the 53rd division on the rim; remove the protractor and join the vertex **O** to the point so marked.

Exercise 14. Measure in degrees the angles **AOB** and **BOC**. Add your results together, and test by measuring the angle **AOC**.

⁎⁎⁎ Angles drawn with arms of sufficient length for use with the protractor should be given for measurement by the teacher.

Exercise 15. Measure the angles **PXQ** and **RXQ**. Find by subtraction the number of degrees in the angle **PXR**. Test your result by measuring that angle.

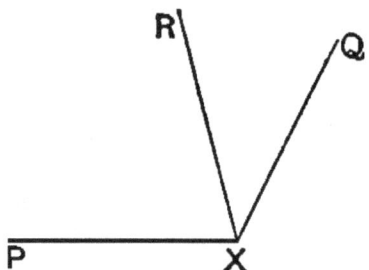

∗∗* *Other diagrams for practice in measuring angles should be provided by the teacher.*

Exercise 16. Draw a straight line **AB** of length 3″. From **A** draw a line making an angle of 62° with **AB**.

From **B** draw a line making an angle of 62° with **BA**. (Both lines are to be drawn on the same side of **AB**.)

Exercise 17. Repeat Exercise 16, but make the angles at **A** and **B** (i) 27°, (ii) 81°, (iii) 157°. (This may be done in a single figure.)

Exercise 18. Draw a straight line **AB** of length 8 cm. From **A** draw two lines, one on each side of **AB**, each making an angle of 47° with it. Repeat the process, making angles of 75° and 131° on each side of **AB**. (This is to be done in a single figure.)

If your figure were folded about **AB**, how would the lines on one side of **AB** fall with regard to those on the other side?

Exercise 19. Draw (i) an acute angle, (ii) an obtuse angle, (iii) a reflex angle.

In each case judge as nearly as you can (without using your protractor) how many degrees there are in the angle.

Check your estimates by measurement, noting your errors; and express these errors as percentages of the measured values.

Tabulate your results as in Exercise 4, p. 17.

ANGLES

Exercise 20. Without using your protractor draw angles as nearly as you can judge to contain 45°, 30°, 78°, 125°, 64°, 115°, 225°.

Measure your attempts, and tabulate the results.

(Adjacent and Vertically Opposite Angles)

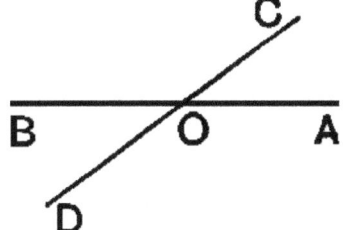

Two angles which have one arm in common, and lie on opposite sides of it, are said to be **adjacent**. Point out four pairs of adjacent angles in the marginal Figure.

The angles **AOC**, **BOD** are said to be **vertically opposite**. Point out another pair of vertically opposite angles.

Exercise 21. Draw a straight line **AB**, and from any point **O** in it draw another line **OC**. Do this three times, placing **OC** in different positions.

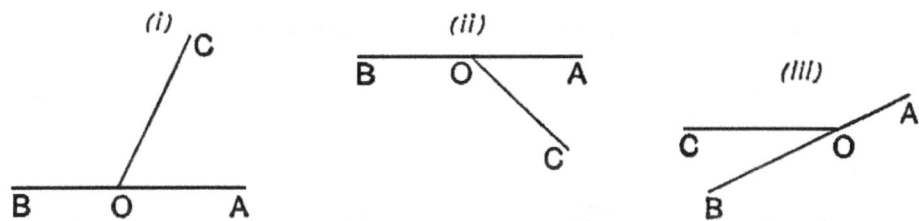

Measure the angle **AOC**; and, without moving the protractor, measure the adjacent angle **BOC**. In each case fill up the form:

∠ **AOC** + ∠ **BOC** =   degrees =   right angles.

Compare the three results, and write down in words the conclusion you draw. Try to explain the reason.

Exercise 22. In the Figures of Exercise 21,

(i) if the ∠ **AOC** = 65°, *reckon* the ∠ **BOC**.

(ii) if the ∠ **BOC** = 140°, *reckon* the ∠ **AOC**.

(iii) if the ∠ **AOC** = 153°, *reckon* the ∠ **BOC**.

Exercise 23. Draw a straight line **OX**. Make the angle **XOP** = 55°; and on the other side of **OX** make the angle **XOQ** = 120°. Are **OP** and **OQ** in one straight line? If not, how should **OQ** be turned, so as to bring it into line with **OP**?

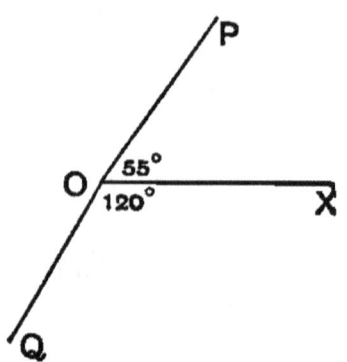

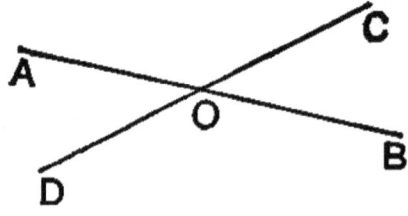

Exercise 24. Draw the straight lines **AB**, **CD** crossing one another at **O**. Measure the angle **AOC**. Hence reckon the angles **BOC**, **AOD**, **DOB**.

Now compare the vertically opposite angles thus:

∠ **BOC** =   degrees   ∠ **AOC** =   degrees

∠ **AOD** =   degrees   ∠ **BOD** =   degrees

Write down your conclusion in words.

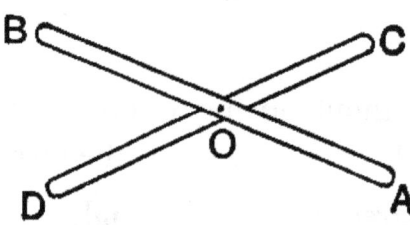

NOTE. The equality of vertically opposite angles should be illustrated by experiment.

For instance: two narrow strips of cardboard may be pivoted by a drawing-pin at **O**. Bring the strips into coincidence, then slowly open them out. Observe that the same movement which opens the angle **AOC**, also opens the angle **BOD**: that is to say, these angles are the result of the *same amount of turning*, and are therefore equal to one another.

ANGLES

Exercise 25. In the Figure of Exercise 24:

(i) If the ∠ **BOD** = 143°,
reckon each of the ∠^{S} **BOC, COA, AOD**.

(ii) If the ∠ **AOD** = 29°,
reckon each of the ∠^{S} **DOB, BOC, COA**.

(iii) If the ∠ **COA** = 137°,
reckon each of the ∠^{S} **BOD, DOA, COB**.

Exercise 26. Draw a straight line **AB**, and from a point **O** in it draw any straight lines **OC, OD**, on the same side of **AB**. Measure the angles **AOC, COD, DOB**, and find their sum. Account for the result.

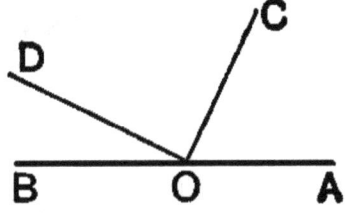

Exercise 27. From a point **O** draw three straight lines **OA, OB, OC**. Measure the angles **AOB, BOC, COA**, and fill up the following:

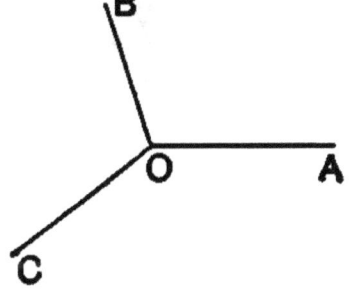

∠ **AOB** + ∠ **BOC** + ∠ **COA**
    =   degrees.
    =   right angles.

Exercise 28. In the Figure of Exercise 27:

(i) If ∠ **AOB** = 125°, and ∠ **BOC** = 82°,
reckon the ∠ **COA**.

(ii) If ∠ **AOB** = 134°, and ∠ **AOC** = 152°,
reckon the ∠ **BOC**.

In each case test by measurement.

CHAPTER VI

ANGLES CONTINUED

CONSTRUCTIONS WITH RULER AND COMPASSES

PROBLEM 2

To draw an angle equal to a given angle **O**.

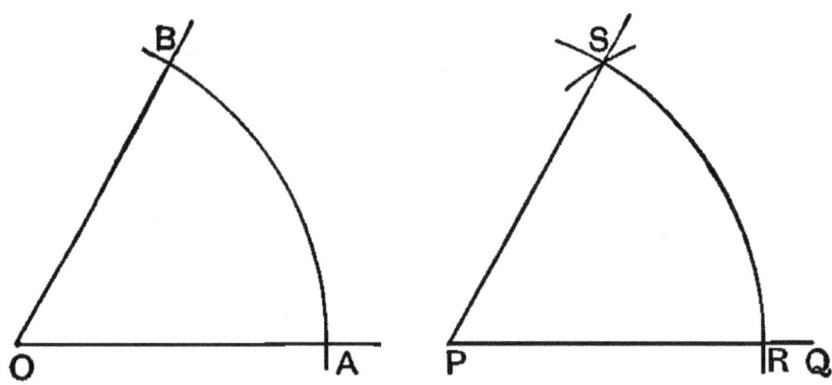

[The angle **O** may be of any size: its arms may be conveniently made about 8 cm. in length.]

Construction. Draw a straight line **PQ**, say about 8 cm. long.

With centre **O**, and any length (say 6 cm.) as radius, draw a circle cutting the arms of the given angle at **A** and **B**.

With centre **P**, and with the *same* radius as before, draw a circle cutting **PQ** at **R**.

(Only arcs of these two circles are shown in the Figure.)

ANGLES CONTINUED

Take in your compasses the distance between the points **A** and **B**, that is to say, the length of the *chord* **AB** (there is no need to draw the chord): with centre **R**, and this length as radius, cut the second circle at **S**.

From **P** draw a straight line through **S**.

Now measure both angles with your protractor, and see if they are equal.

(Further Tests)

(i) Trace the ∠ **QPS**, and see if the tracing can be made to coincide with, that is, *exactly fit over* the given ∠ **O**.

(ii) Now, having found by experiment that the two angles are equal, let us see *why* they are equal. In the equal circles, whose centres are at **O** and **P**, you measured off equal *chords*, though you did not draw them. Are the *arcs* **RS**, **AB** equal? How do you know this? And we have found by experiment (p. 32) that in equal circles, by joining the ends of equal arcs to the centres, we make equal angles.

(iii) Would the ∠ **RPS** have come out equal to the ∠ **O**, if you had drawn the two circles with *different radii*. Try: make the circle with centre **O** larger than the circle with centre **P**, but otherwise work as before. Are the angles at **P** and **O** equal now? Then which is greater?

Exercise 1. Draw an angle of 73° with your protractor. Then, with ruler and compasses only, construct an equal angle. Test your drawing with the protractor.

Exercise 2. Repeat the last Exercise with an angle of 126°.

Exercise 3. Draw an angle **AOB** of any size. Then, with ruler and compasses, draw a line **OC** making the ∠ **AOC** equal to the ∠ **AOB** on the other side of **OC**. Test with tracing-paper.

Exercise 4. Draw an angle of 35° with your protractor; then, with ruler and compasses, construct another angle *three times* the size of the first. Test your construction by measurement.

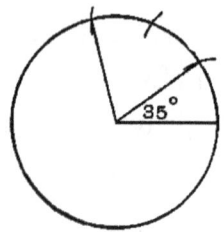

Exercise 5. I want to draw an angle *five times* as great as a given angle **A**. Explain in your own words how this may be done.

Exercise 6. Draw a circle with centre **O** and *any* radius. Step off this radius from **A** to **B** on the circumference, and join **OA, OB**.

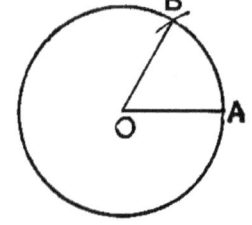

What fraction is the ∠ **AOB** of *four right angles*, and why? How many degrees are there in the ∠ **AOB**? Answer, then test by measurement.

Exercise 7. Draw an angle of 120°, using ruler and compasses only.

Exercise 8. With your protractor draw a *right angle* **AOB**. With centre **O** and any radius (say 7 cm.) draw the arc **AB**. What part of the whole circumference is this arc?

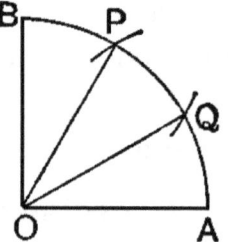

From centre **A**, with *the same radius*, cut the arc at **P**; and from centre **B**, with the same radius cut the arc at **Q**. Join **OP, OQ**.

How large are the ∠ˢ **AOQ, QOP, POB**? Answer, giving your reason: then measure.

ANGLES CONTINUED

(Bisection of Angles)

Draw an angle of any size on tracing paper, and fold it so as to bring one arm exactly over the other. Unfold your paper, and mark the crease. The crease **bisects** the angle, that is, divides it into two equal parts. Why?

How would you bisect an angle by means of your protractor?

PROBLEM 3

To bisect an angle **AOB** *with ruler and compasses.*

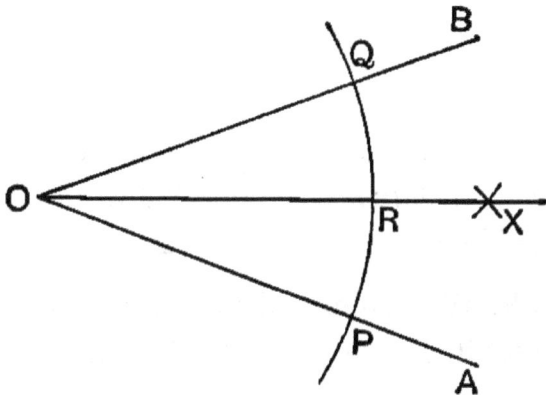

[The given angle **AOB** may be of any size: its arms may be conveniently taken about 9 cm. in length.]

Construction. With centre **O**, and any radius, draw an arc of a circle cutting **OA** at **P** and **OB** at **Q**.

Take in your compasses any length greater than half the distance from **P** to **Q**.

With centre **P**, and this length as radius, draw an arc. With centre **Q**, and *the same radius*, draw another arc, cutting the former at **X**.

Join **OX**. Now, with your protractor, measure each of the angles **AOX**, **BOX**, and see if they are equal.

EXPERIMENTAL AND PRACTICAL GEOMETRY

(Further Tests)

(i) By means of tracing-paper, or by folding about **OX**, ascertain if the ∠ **AOX** = the ∠ **BOX**.

(ii) Put **R** where **OX** cuts the arc **PQ**. Compare with your dividers the distances (chords) **RP**, **RQ**. Are they equal? If so, how does this prove that the ∠^{S} **AOX**, **BOX** are equal?

(iii) If the arc drawn from centre **P** had a greater radius than that drawn from centre **Q**, would **OX** still be the bisector of the ∠ **AOB**? If not, towards which arm would **OX** lean?

You see then that **OX** is the bisector in our problem because we have worked from the arms **OA** and **OB** in exactly the same way.

(iv) In drawing the arcs from **P** and **Q** as centres, why did we take a radius *greater than half* **PQ**? What would have happened if the radius had been *less* than half **PQ**?

Exercise 9. With ruler and compasses only, draw an angle of 60°, and bisect it. Test your work with the protractor.

Exercise 10. Draw an angle of 150° with your protractor; then with ruler and compasses, divide the angle into *four* equal parts.

Exercise 11. With ruler and compasses construct an angle of 60°; then obtain from it an angle of 15°.

Exercise 12. Draw a straight line **AB**. In **AB** take a point **O**, and from it draw a line **OC** making any angle with **OA**. Bisect the angles **AOC**, **BOC** *(by construction)*, and call the bisectors **OX** and **OY**. Measure the angle **XOY**. Can you account for the result?

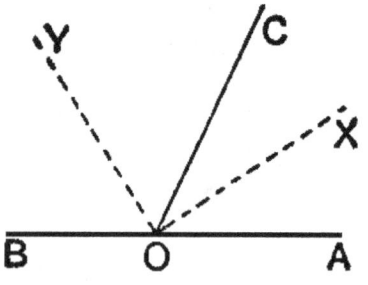

Exercise 13. Draw two straight lines **AB**, **CD** crossing one another at **O** at any angle. Bisect the angles **BOD**, **AOC** *(by construction)*. Call the bisectors **OX** and **OY**. What do you notice as to the direction of these two bisectors?

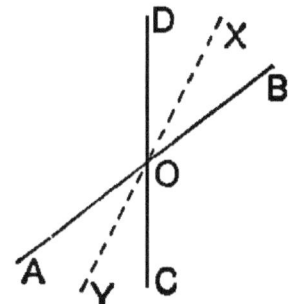

Exercise 14. Draw the patterns shown below:

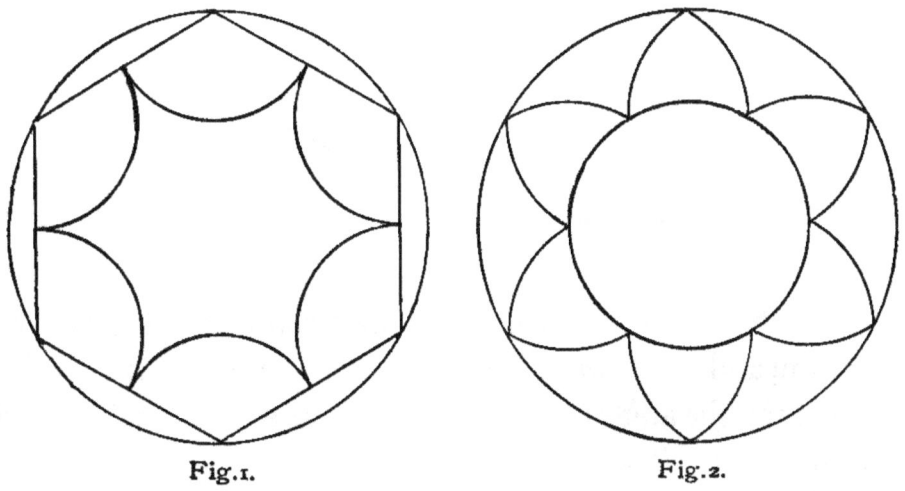

Fig. 1.   Fig. 2.

(i) In Figure 1. The circle is to be drawn first, radius 5 cm.

(ii) In Figure 2. The *inner* circle is to be drawn first, radius 3 cm., the arcs of the star are to be of the same radius.

CHAPTER VII

DIRECTION, PARALLELS

Suppose a man is walking along a straight path from **A** towards **B**; and suppose that, on reaching the point **P**, he alters his course, and proceeds along the path **PC**.

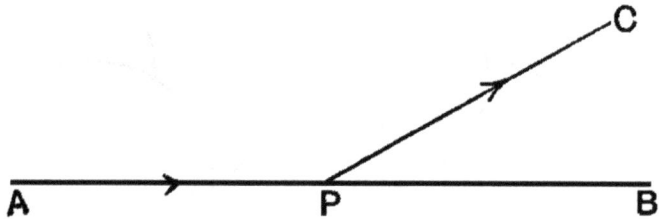

Then **AB** represents his first direction, **PC** his second direction; and his *change of direction* is given by the angle **BPC**, that is to say, the angle between his new course and *the line which he would have followed if he had gone straight on*.

Exercise 1. A ship sailing due East alters her course 25° towards North. Draw a diagram to represent this, marking the angle which shows her change of direction.

Exercise 2. A man walks due South, then turns 43° towards West. Show by a Figure his first direction, his second direction, and his change of direction.

Two men are walking from **A** towards **B**. One on arriving at **P** changes his direction, say by 37°, to his left, following the line **PC**. The other goes straight on to **Q**, then also changes his direction by 37° to his left, following the line **QD**.

DIRECTION, PARALLELS

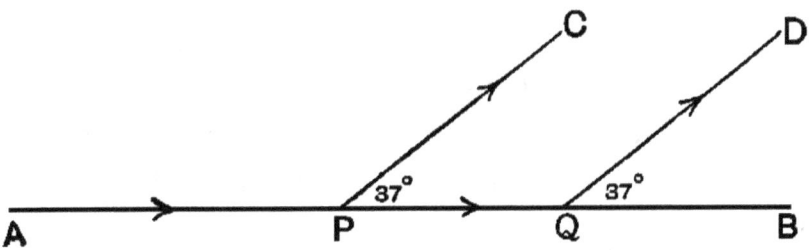

Do the two new paths meet? Does it seem to you that they would meet if they were prolonged ever so far forwards or backwards? Lines such as **PC** and **QD**, *which point in the same direction* never meet: they are said to be **parallel**; and the angles **BPC, BQD**, which fix the direction of these lines by comparison with **AB**, are called **corresponding angles**.

You have now to learn the use of the triangular rulers called **set squares**. Notice that one angle in each is a *right angle*: the remaining angles in one set square are both 45°; in the other they are 60° and 30°.

With a set square and a straight ruler we can draw parallel lines, as follows:

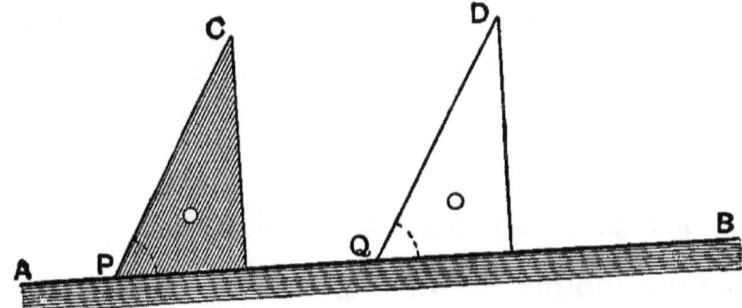

Place either set square in any position such as that shaded in the diagram, and against one of its sides lay a straight ruler (marked **AB** in the Figure). Holding the ruler firm, slide the set square along it, so that the side marked **PC** moves into the position **QD**. Then **QD** and **PC** are parallel. Why? Thus, if in any two positions of the set square we rule lines along the same edge, we get a pair of parallels.

EXPERIMENTAL AND PRACTICAL GEOMETRY

Before going further practise yourself a little in this process, drawing pairs of parallel lines in various positions and directions. If the straight ruler has a bevelled edge, the set square is apt to slip up over it: in this case use the longest side of your other set square as a guide.

Exercise 3. Draw with your set squares two parallel lines **AB**, **CD**, about 10 cm. long and about 5 cm. apart. Draw *any* straight line **EF** across them, and number the angles so formed as in the diagram below.

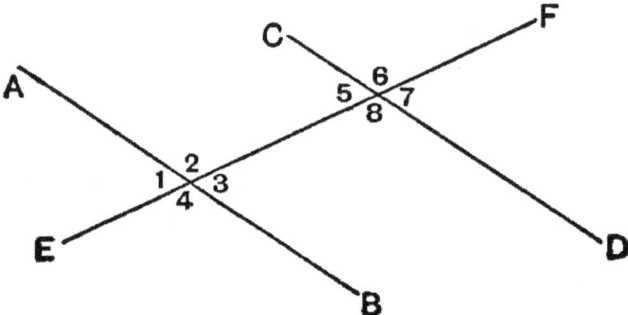

(i) Point out four pairs of **corresponding** angles.

Carefully measure each pair of corresponding angles with your protractor, and enter their values in your Figure. Having drawn **EF** at random your measurements show that *corresponding angles* in each pair *are equal*. Note this.

(ii) The angles 3 and 5 are said to be **alternate**.

Point out another pair of alternate angles.

Looking back to your previous measurements, do you find alternate angles equal?

We may account for this by what has gone before, as follows:

The angle 5 = the angle 1. Why?

The angle 3 = the angle 1. Why?

Hence we see that the angle 5 must be equal to the angle 3.

DIRECTION, PARALLELS

(iii) The angles 3 and 8 are called **interior** angles.

Add together the angles 3 and 8.

Add together the angles 2 and 5.

Compare the results and try to account for them.

(iv) Put **P** and **Q** at the points where **EF** cuts the parallels **AB**, **CD**; then make a tracing of your figure. Move the tracing-paper so that the trace of **EF** slides along the original line **EF**, until the trace of **P** falls on **Q**. Where does the trace of **AB** fall? In this way verify the conclusions marked (i) and (iii).

Again slide your tracing-paper round until the trace of **P** falls on **Q**, and the trace of **Q** on **P**. Where do the traces of **AB** and **CD** fall? In this way verify the conclusion marked (ii).

Exercise 4. Draw two parallels **AB**, **CD**; and cut them by a line **EF**, making an angle of 57° with **AB**. Call this angle 1, and number the rest as before. Now write down (without measurement) the number of degrees in each of the angles 2, 3, 4, 5, 6, 7, 8.

Exercise 5. Repeat the last Exercise, drawing **EF** at an angle of 117° with **AB**. Write down (without measuring) the remaining angles.

Exercise 6. Draw a line **AB** about 3½″ long. Take a point **P** about 2″ from **AB**. From **A** draw a line through **P**, and measure the angle **PAB**. Now, using your protractor, draw a line through **P** parallel to **AB**. Do this in two ways: (i) by making *corresponding* angles equal; (ii) by making *alternate* angles equal.

EXPERIMENTAL AND PRACTICAL GEOMETRY

PROBLEM 4

Through a given point **P** *to draw* **with a set square** *a line parallel to a given straight line* **AB**.

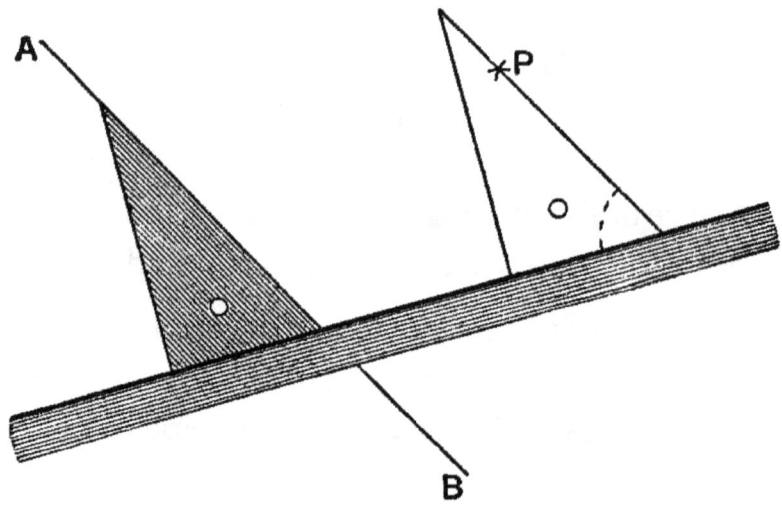

Place either set square so that one of its sides lies along **AB** in the position shaded in the diagram.

Against either of the other sides lay a straight-edge (either a straight ruler or the longest side of the second set square).

Then holding the straight-edge firmly, slide the set square along it until the side originally placed along **AB** passes through the point **P**.

A line ruled along this side is parallel to **AB**, for the *corresponding angles* marked in the diagram are necessarily equal.

DIRECTION, PARALLELS

PROBLEM 5

Through a given point **P** *to draw* **with ruler and compasses** *a line parallel to a given straight line* **AB**.

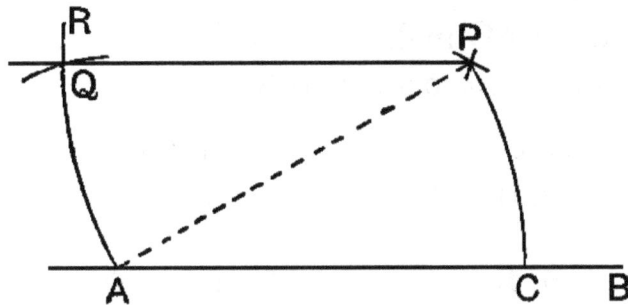

[A convenient figure is got by making **AB** about 8 cm. long, and placing **P** about 5 cm. from **AB**.]

Construction. With **A** (or any other point in **AB**) as centre, and the distance **AP** as radius, draw an arc cutting **AB** at **C**.

With **P** as centre, and the *same radius* **PA**, draw the arc **AR**.

Take the distance (or chord) **PC** in your compasses, and with centre **A** cut the arc **AR** at **Q**.

Join **PQ**.

Now test to see if **PQ** is parallel to **AB**.

(Tests)

(i) Join **AP**, and ascertain by any practical means if the alternate angles **CAP**, **QPA** are equal. If so, **AB** and **PQ** are parallel.

(ii) Could you not conclude without measurement that the ∠ **CAP** = the ∠ **QPA**? Bear in mind that the arcs **CP**, **QA** have the same radius; that is, they are arcs of equal circles. Also remember that the arc **AQ** has been got by stepping off a chord equal to the chord **PC**. Now argue the rest out for yourself.

EXPERIMENTAL AND PRACTICAL GEOMETRY

Exercise 7. Take two points **A** and **B**, 6 cm. apart. Through **A** draw any straight line; and through **B** draw a parallel line with your set squares.

Exercise 8. Draw a line **AB** of length 3″. With your protractor draw **AC** making an angle of 76° with **AB**. Now through **B** draw a line parallel to **AC**.

Do this Exercise twice, drawing the parallel (i) with set squares; (ii) with ruler and compasses.

Exercise 9. Repeat Exercise 8, making **AB** of length 9 cm., and the ∠ **BAC** equal to 32°. Draw the parallel with your set squares; then test with ruler and compasses (by going through the construction of Problem 5).

Exercise 10. Draw a right angle **AOB** with your protractor, making each of the arms **OA**, **OB** 7.5 cm. in length. Through **A** draw a parallel to **OB**, and through **B** draw a parallel to **OA**. Do this with set squares.

What is the shape of the figure you have just drawn?

Exercise 11. Draw a straight line **AB** of length 7 cm. Find a point **P** that is 7 cm. from **A** and also 7 cm. from **B**. Through **P** draw a parallel to **AB**. (All this is to be done with ruler and compasses.)

Exercise 12. Draw a line **AC**, 2″ long, and bisect it by measurement at **B**. Through **A**, **B**, **C** draw parallels **AX**, **BY**, **CZ** in any direction (with set squares). Now draw any line across the parallels cutting them at **P**, **Q**, and **R**. Measure and compare **PQ** and **QR**.

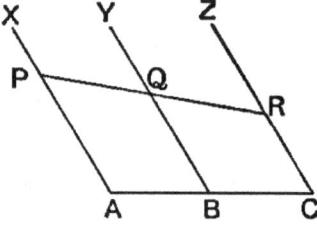

Draw any other line across the parallels cutting them at **L**, **M**, and **N**. Measure and compare **LM** and **MN**.

What conclusion do you arrive at from these experiments?

PROBLEM 6

*To divide a given straight line **AB** into five equal parts (without measurement).*

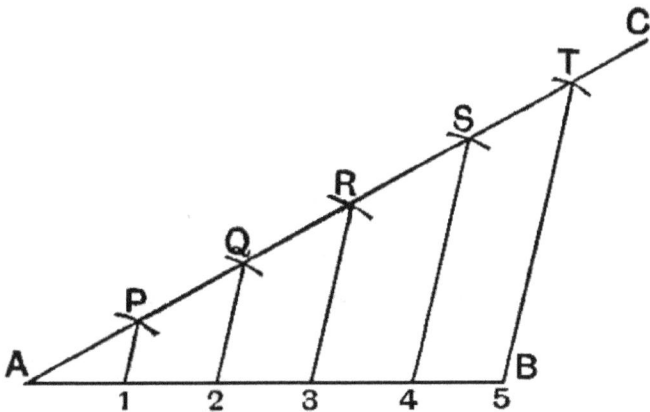

[The given line **AB** may be of any length; but do not measure it.]

Construction. From **A** draw **AC**, making any angle with **AB**.

Take any length in your compasses, and step it off *five* times along **AC**. Call the points of division **P, Q, R, S, T**.

Join **TB**.

Through **P, Q, R, S** draw parallels to **TB** (with set squares).

These parallels will divide **AB** into *five* equal parts. Test this with your dividers.

In the same way a straight line may be divided into *three*, *seven*, or any other number of equal parts.

The construction depends on the law which you will have found out from Exercise 12.

Exercise 13. Draw a line 2.7″ long, and divide it by the last construction into three equal parts. Test afterwards by measurement.

Exercise 14. Use the above method to *bisect* a line of 7.8 cm. Bisect the same line by Problem 1, p. 23, and see if your two results agree.

Exercise 15. Draw a line 3.2″ long, and divide it by the above construction into *four* equal parts.

How else could you divide a line into four equal parts, using ruler and compasses only?

Exercise 16. Draw a line 9 cm. long, and divide it into *seven* equal parts. Test with your dividers.

Exercise 17. From a line 3.5″ long, cut off *one-fifth* part by construction.

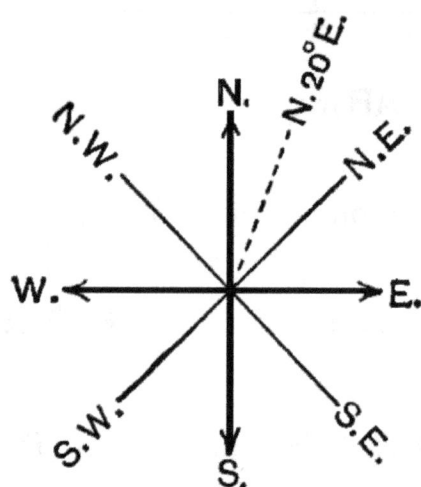

The line of direction which bisects the angle between North and East, is called *North-East*; and the terms North-West, South-East, South-West, have corresponding meanings.

DIRECTION, PARALLELS

If, looking from a light-house, a ship is seen in the direction North-West, we say that it *bears* N.W. from the light-house, or that its *bearing* is N.W. If the direction of the ship, as seen from the light-house, makes with the line pointing North an angle of 20° on the East side of that line, we say that the ship bears 20° East of North, or N. 20° E.

Exercise 18. A man walks 6 kilometres due East, then 5 kilometres due North. Draw a plan (scale 1 km. to 1 cm.), and find by measurement how far he is from his starting-point.

Exercise 19. North West from my garden gate is a cottage, 300 yards distant: North East of the cottage and 250 yards from it is a well. Draw a plan (scale 100 yards to 1 inch), and find as nearly as you can how far the well is from the garden gate.

Exercise 20. Two cyclists, each riding 14 km. an hour, leave a house at the same time. One goes by a straight road leading S.E.; the other by a road leading S.W. How far apart will they be in half an hour? (Scale 1 km. to 1 cm.)

Exercise 21. A man goes South 4 miles, then West 6 miles, then South again 4 miles. How far is he now from his starting-point? (Scale 2 miles to 1 inch.)

Exercise 22. A ship on leaving port sails N.W. for 18 miles then North for 15 miles. Show her course on the scale of 10 miles to 1 inch. Find her approximate distance, and her bearing from the port, that is, how many degrees West of North.

Exercise 23. A boy walks 200 yards in a certain direction; then, turning 68° to his left, he walks 300 yards; finally he turns 68° to his right, and walks 250 yards. Show his track on a plan (100 yards to 1 inch); and explain why his third direction is parallel to his first. How far is he at last from his starting-point?

EXPERIMENTAL AND PRACTICAL GEOMETRY

Exercise 24. A traveller wishes to go due North, but finds his way barred by a swamp. He therefore walks 5 kilometres N.E., then 5 kilometres North, then 5 kilometres N.W.; and now he finds himself due North of his starting-point. How many kilometres has he lost by having gone out of his way? (Scale 1 km. to 1 cm.)

Exercise 25. Draw the patterns given below: the dimensions should be twice those of the copies.

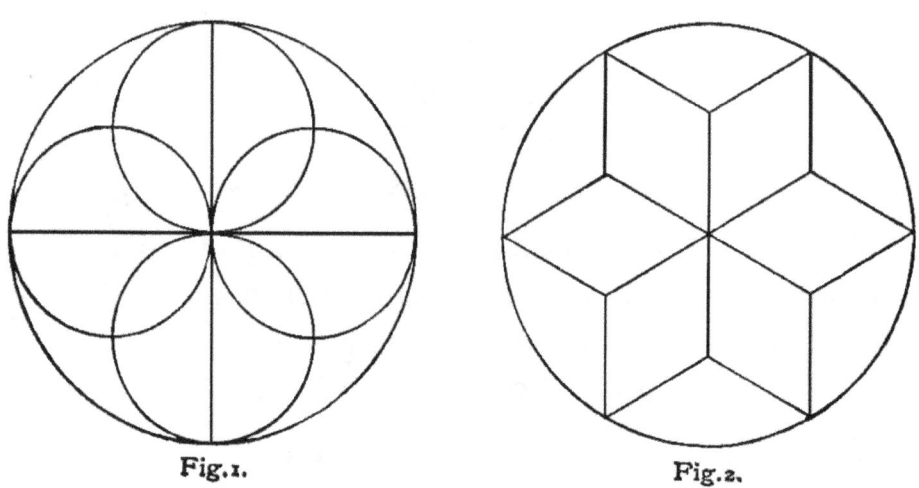

Fig. 1.   Fig. 2.

CHAPTER VIII

PERPENDICULARS

PROBLEM 7

To draw **with ruler and compasses** *a straight line bisecting a given straight line* **AB** *at right angles.*

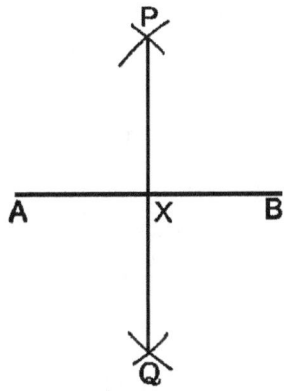

Construction. Follow the method of Problem 1, p. 23.

Your experiments have already shown that **PQ** cuts **AB** at its middle point. We have now to satisfy ourselves that **PQ** is at right angles, or perpendicular to **AB**. Test this first with your protractor.

(Further Tests)

(i) Make a tracing of your figure, and fold it so as to bring **A** over **B**. Note the position of the crease, and explain the result.

(ii) Make a tracing as before, and turn it about the point **X** until the trace of **XA** lies along **XP**. Where does the trace of **XP** fall? Show from this that **PQ** is at right angles to **AB**.

Exercise 1. Draw a straight line **AB**, 8 cm. long, and bisect it at right angles by a line **PQ**. Use radii of length 5 cm.; and measure **PQ**.

Exercise 2. Draw a line of any length, say 2.4″, on tracing paper; and bisect it at right angles by **PQ**, choosing your own radii for the arcs.

Show by measurement that **PQ** bisects **AB**, *and also that* **AB** *bisects* **PQ**.

If you fold the figure about **PQ** where will the point **A** fall?

If you fold the figure about **AB** where will the point **P** fall?

The figure is *symmetrical* about **PQ**; and also about **AB**.

Exercise 3. Take a line **AB** of length 7 cm. With centre **A** and radius 5 cm. draw a circle. With centre **B** and radius 4 cm. draw a circle cutting the first at **P** and **Q**. Join **PQ**. "Then **PQ** bisects **AB** at *right angles*." Which part of this statement is true? Which part is false?

Exercise 4. Draw a line **AB** of any length you like, and bisect it at right angles by **PQ**, choosing the radii yourself: note the length of the radii you use.

How far is **P** from **A** and **B**? How far is **Q** from **A** and **B**?

Take *any* point in **PQ**, and call it **R**. Measure **RA** and **RB**, and compare their lengths. You will find that **R** is *equidistant* from **A** and **B**.

PERPENDICULARS

Exercise 5. Draw a line **AB**, 8 cm. long. With your compasses find two points **P** and **Q** distant 7 cm. from both **A** and **B**; also two points **R** and **S** distant 6 cm. from both **A** and **B**; also two points **X** and **Y** distant 5 cm. from both **A** and **B**. On what line do all these points lie? How many points are there which are 4 cm. from both **A** and **B**?

PROBLEM 8

*Through a given point **P** to draw* **with set squares** *a line* **perpendicular** *to a given straight line* **AB**.

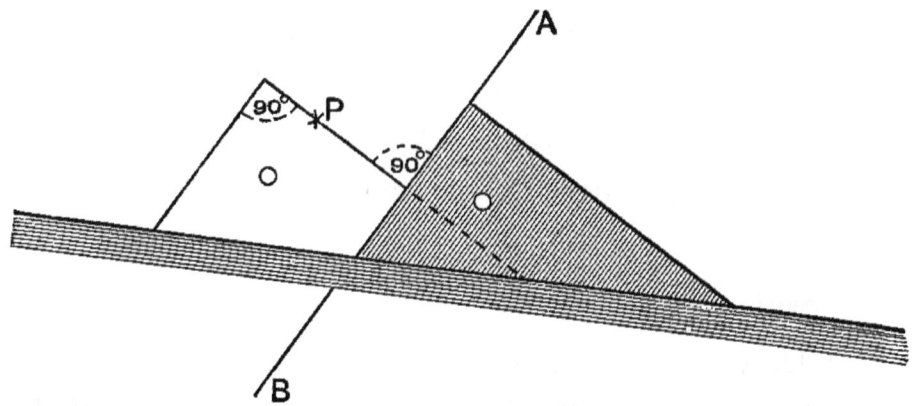

Take either set square and place one of the sides containing the right angle along **AB**.

Apply the straight-edge to the longest side (*i.e.* the side opposite the right angle) of the set square; and slide the latter until the side originally perpendicular to **AB** passes through **P**.

A line ruled along this side will be perpendicular to **AB**, for the alternate angles marked in the diagram are equal.

NOTE. Following the principle of this method, you should devise for yourself arrangements of a set square and straight edge by which a line may be drawn through a given point **P** making with a given line **AB** an angle (i) of 45°, (ii) of 60°, (iii) of 30°.

EXPERIMENTAL AND PRACTICAL GEOMETRY

(Exercises to be done with Set Squares)

Exercise 6. Draw a straight line **AX**, and mark off along it **AB**, **BC**, **CD**, each 1″ in length. Through **A**, **B**, **C**, and **D** draw lines perpendicular to **AX**. Why are these lines parallel?

Exercise 7. Draw a line **AB** of length 7 cm. Through **A** draw a perpendicular to **AB**, and along it measure **AC** 7 cm. long. Through **B** draw a parallel to **AC**; and through **C** draw a parallel to **AB**.

What is the shape of the figure you have thus drawn?

Exercise 8. Draw a line **AB**, 8 cm. long. Draw **AC** perpendicular to **AB**, and make **AC** = 6 cm. Join **BC**. From **A** draw **AD** perpendicular to **AC**. Measure **AD**.

Exercise 9. Draw a line **AB**. At **A** make (with your set squares) (i) a right angle, (ii) an angle of 60°, (iii) an angle of 30°, (iv) an angle of 45°.

Exercise 10.

(a) Draw a line **AB** of length 10.5 cm. From **A** (with your protractor) draw **AC** and **AD** making angles of 45° with **AB**, one on each side. Through **B** draw (with set squares) parallels to **AC** and **AD**.

What is the shape of the figure you have thus drawn?

(b) Take a line **AB**, 6 cm. long. Using a radius also of 6 cm., bisect **AB** at right angles by **PQ**. From centre **X** (the point of bisection) with radius 3 cm. mark off points **C** and **D** in **PQ**. Join **CA**, **CB**, **DA**, **DB**.

What is the shape of the figure **ACBD**? Measure the angles **DAC**, **ACB**.

(c) Make a straight line **BC** of length 7.6 cm.; and through **B** and **C** draw two parallels **BP**, **CQ**, (with set squares) in any direction. Bisect the angles **PBC**, **QCB** by lines meeting at **A**, and measure the angle **BAC**.

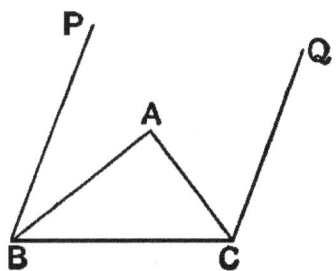

PROBLEM 9, FIRST METHOD

To draw, **with ruler and compasses**, *a straight line* **perpendicular** *to a given straight line* **AB** *at a given point* **X** *in it.*

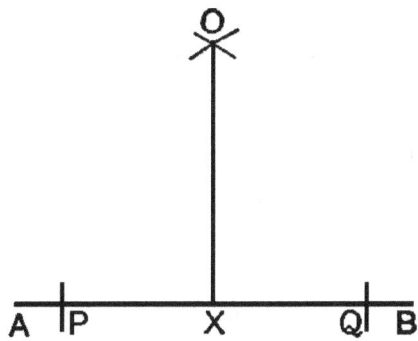

[The given straight line **AB** may be of any length, for convenience say about 4″. The given point **X** in this construction should not be taken near an end of **AB**: take **X** about 1.5″ from **A**.]

Construction. Take in your compasses any length less than **XA** (say a little over 1″), and with **X** as centre mark off two points **P** and **Q** in **AB**.

Now take in your compasses any length greater than **PX** (say about 2″), and first with **P** as centre, then with **Q** as centre, draw two arcs cutting at **O**.

Join **OX**.

Now test with your protractor to see if **OX** is perpendicular to **AB**.

EXPERIMENTAL AND PRACTICAL GEOMETRY

(Further Tests)

(i) Test with a set square and straight-edge as explained in Problem 8, p. 57.

(ii) Use the test marked (ii) in Problem 7, p. 55.

(iii) Invent a test with ruler and compasses to find if the angles **OXP**, **OXQ** are equal. (See Problem 2, p. 38.) If they are, how does this show that **OX** is perpendicular to **AB**?

PROBLEM 9, SECOND METHOD

[When the given point **X** is at or near one end of **AB**.]

Construction. With **X** as centre, and any length as radius, draw the arc **CDE**, cutting **AB** at **C**.

With the *same radius* step off from **C** the points **D** and **E** round the arc.

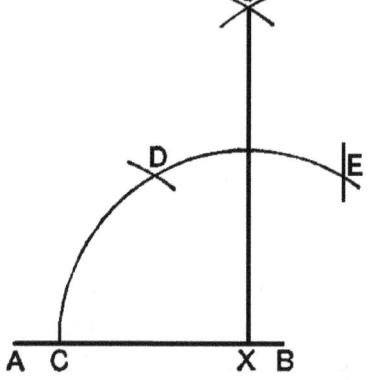

With **D** and **E** as centres, and the same radius as before, draw arcs cutting at **O**.

Join **XO**.

(Verification)

Join **DX** and **EX**.

How many degrees are there in the ∠^{S} **CXD**, **DXE**? Why? [p. 24.]

How many degrees are there in the ∠^{S} **DXO**, **EXO**? Why? [p. 41.]

How many degrees are there in the ∠ **AXO**?

PERPENDICULARS

(Perpendiculars by Construction)

Exercise 11. Draw a straight line 4″ long. At points 1½″ from each end erect perpendiculars (First Method). Why are these parallel?

Exercise 12. Draw a line **AB**, 6 cm. long. At each end erect perpendiculars **AC**, **BD** (Second Method), each 6 cm. long. Join **CD**.

Name any test by which you can find if **CD** is parallel to **AB**.

Exercise 13. Employ Problem 9 (Second Method) and Problem 3 (p. 41) to draw lines making with a given line **AB** angles of 90°, 45°, 22½°.

Exercise 14. By constructions with ruler and compasses draw lines making angles of 60°, 30°, 15° with a given line **AB**.

How would you draw a *reflex* angle of (i) 270°, (ii) 300°?

Exercise 15. Construct a perpendicular at the end **A** of a given line **AB**. Then, with ruler and compasses, draw **AC** making an angle of 135° with **AB**.

PROBLEM 10

To draw **with ruler and compasses** *a straight line* **perpendicular** *to a given line* **AB** *from a given point* **X** *outside it.*

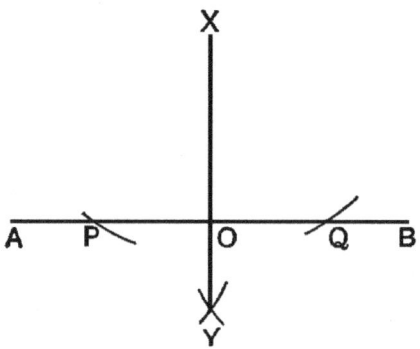

[The given line **AB** may be taken about 4″ long.]

Construction. With centre **X**, and any radius of sufficient length, cut **AB** at **P** and **Q**.

Take in your compasses any length greater than half **PQ**.

With centre **P**, and this length as radius, draw an arc on the side of **AB** opposite **X**;

With centre **Q**, and the *same radius*, draw an arc cutting the last arc at Y.

Join **XY**, cutting **AB** at **O**.

Now apply any of the tests previously explained to ascertain if **XO** is perpendicular to **AB**.

Exercise 16. With your set square or protractor draw a right angle **AOB**; and make **OA** = 7.5 cm., and **OB** = 5.5 cm. Join **AB**, and by construction drop a perpendicular on **AB** from **O**.

Exercise 17. Draw a line **AB** of length 1.6″. Find with your compasses a point **P** distant 1.7″ from both **A** and **B**. From **P** drop a perpendicular **PM** on **AB** (by construction). Measure **PM**.

Exercise 18. Draw a straight line **AB**, and take any point **P** outside it. Draw **PX** perpendicular to **AB** (with set squares). Measure **PX**.

Now take any two points **Y**, **Z** in **AB** on the same side of **X**. Join and measure **PY**, **PZ**.

Of the lines **PX**, **PY**, **PZ**, which is least? Which is greatest? Can you draw from **P** to **AB** a shorter line than the perpendicular **PX**?

The distance of a point **P** from a straight line **AB** is understood to be the *length of the perpendicular* **PX**, this being the shortest line that can be drawn from **P** to **AB**.

Exercise 19. Take a point **O** outside a straight line **AB**, and from **O** draw **OX** perpendicular to **AB** (with set squares).

With centre **O** draw three concentric circles: the radius of the first is to be *less than* **OX**; the radius of the second is to be *equal to* **OX**; the radius of the third is to be *greater than* **OX**.

Now carefully notice if, and how, these circles meet **AB**. What conclusion do you draw?

A circle drawn with a given point **O** as centre will *touch* a given line **AB** if its radius is equal to the perpendicular from **O** to **AB**.

If the radius is greater than this perpendicular, the circle will cut **AB** in two points; if less, the circle will not meet **AB** at all.

EXPERIMENTAL AND PRACTICAL GEOMETRY

Exercise 20. Draw the patterns shown below. Your drawings should be twice the size of the copies.

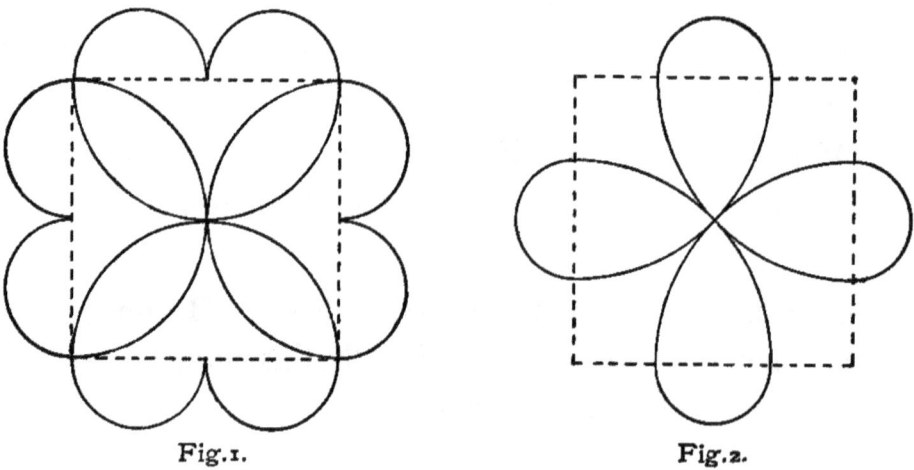

Fig. 1.   Fig. 2.

In Figure 1. the square is drawn first, and the curves are all semi-circles.

In Figure 2. the square is drawn first. The inner arcs are drawn from the vertices of the square as centres, and half the diagonal as radius: the other curves are semi-circles.

CHAPTER IX

TRIANGLES

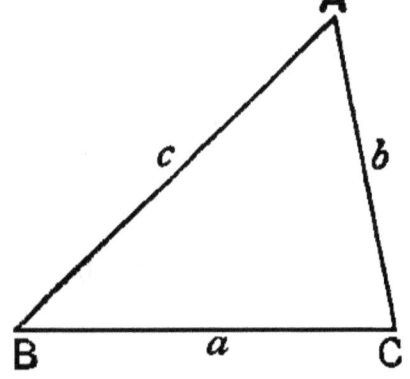

Take any three points **A**, **B**, and **C** not all in a straight line, and join **AB**, **BC**, **CA**. The figure thus formed is called a **triangle**: it has three vertices, three sides, and three angles.

The letters **A**, **B**, **C** are used not only to name the vertices, but to represent the size of the corresponding angles as measured in degrees; while *a, b, c* are taken to represent the lengths of the opposite sides.

Thus in the Figure

A = 58°, **B** = 44°, **C** = 78°;

a = 5.2 cm., b = 4.2 cm., c = 6.0 cm.

The symbol △ is used as an abbreviation for the word *triangle*.

Suppose the Figure represents a triangular field, and you wish to walk from the corner **B** to the corner **C**. Which would be the longer way, to go from **B** to **A** and then from **A** to **C**, or to go straight from **B** to **C** along the side **BC**?

Which is the greater, **AB** + **BC**, or **AC**?

Which is the greater, **BC** + **CA**, or **BA**?

You see at once that *any two sides of a triangle must be together greater than the third side*. Indeed we have already seen the truth of this; for in the first chapter we observed that *the straight line joining two points is the shortest distance between them*.

Exercise 1. To illustrate this further, draw any triangle **ABC**; measure its sides, and fill up the following form:

$a+b=$	cm.	$b+c=$	cm.	$c+a=$	cm.
$c=$	cm.	$a=$	cm.	$b=$	cm.
Excess =	cm.	Excess =	cm.	Excess =	cm.

PROBLEM 11

To draw a triangle, having given the **three sides**.
(For instance: a = 8 cm., b = 7 cm., c = 6 cm.)

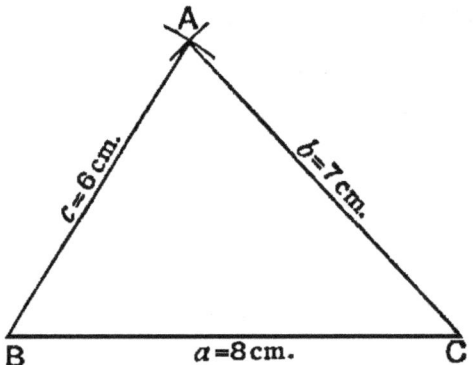

Construction. Draw a straight line **BC** of length 8 cm.

With centre **B**, and a radius of 6 cm. (the length of *c*), draw a circle.

With centre **C**, and a radius of 7 cm. (the length of *b*), draw a second circle cutting the first at **A**.

(*Arcs* of these circles, showing the cutting point, are enough in practice.)

TRIANGLES

Join **AB** and **AC**.

Then **ABC** is the triangle required.

(Remarks)

(i) Notice that the problem is the same as that of finding a point **A** distant 6 cm. from **B**, and 7 cm. from **C**. Can more than one such point be found?

(ii) Draw *two* triangles, one on each side of **BC**, having the dimensions given above.

Cut out the double figure so formed, and fold it about **BC**. What do you find? Are the two triangles of the same size and shape?

(iii) Go through the construction of Problem 11 with the following dimensions: $a = 8$ cm., $b = 4$ cm., $c = 3$ cm.

What difficulty arises? Why is the construction impossible?

(iv) Go through the construction with these dimensions: $a = 8$ cm., $b = 5$ cm., $c = 3$ cm.

Observe carefully what happens, and give a reason for it. Can you draw a triangle whose sides have these lengths?

Exercise 2. Construct (or try to construct) triangles whose sides have the following lengths.

If any set of lengths seems to you impossible, carry out the construction as far as it can go, and then say how and why it fails.

(i) $a = 3.0''$, $b = 3.0''$, $c = 3.0''$.

(ii) $a = 3.0''$, $b = 2.5''$, $c = 2.5''$.

(iii) $a = 3.0''$, $b = 2.5''$, $c = 2.0''$.

(iv) $a = 3.0''$, $b = 1.5''$, $c = 1.0''$.

(v) $a = 3.0''$, $b = 2.0''$, $c = 1.0''$.

EXPERIMENTAL AND PRACTICAL GEOMETRY

(vi) $a = 5.4$ cm, $b = 7.6$ cm, $c = 5.4$ cm.

(vii) $a = 4.5$ cm, $b = 7.0$ cm, $c = 3.5$ cm.

(viii) $a = 4.5$ cm, $b = 7.0$ cm, $c = 2.0$ cm.

(ix) $a = 4.5$ cm, $b = 7.0$ cm, $c = 2.5$ cm.

(x) $a = 5.4$ cm, $b = 8.2$ cm, $c = 4.3$ cm.

In each of the above triangles, when possible, measure all the angles very carefully, and enter the measurements on your drawings: these measurements will be wanted later on.

If a triangle has *all* its sides equal,
> it is said to be **equilateral**;

> if it has *two* sides equal,
>> it is called **isosceles**;

> if none of the sides are equal,
>> it is called **scalene**.

Exercise 3. Point out examples from the triangles you have just drawn of equilateral, isosceles, and scalene triangles. Notice their shapes carefully.

In an isosceles triangle *the vertex* is usually understood to be the point at which the *equal* sides meet; then the opposite side is called the **base**.

(Comparison of Sides and Angles)

Exercise 4. Measure the angles of the equilateral triangle you have drawn in Exercise 2 (i). Are the angles equal? How many degrees are there in each?

Draw any larger or smaller equilateral triangle, and measure its angles. Do you find that equilateral triangles of different sizes have the same shape?

TRIANGLES

Exercise 5. Take the isosceles triangle you have drawn in Exercise 2 (ii), Measure and compare the *base angles*, namely those at **B** and **C**, which are opposite to the equal sides.

Draw *any* isosceles triangle **ABC** (**A** at the vertex) without measuring the sides: measure and compare the angles at the base.

Make a tracing of your triangle; turn the tracing over, and see if it can thus be fitted over the original triangle **ABC**. If so, where does the trace of the ∠ **B** fall? And where does the trace of the ∠ **C** fall?

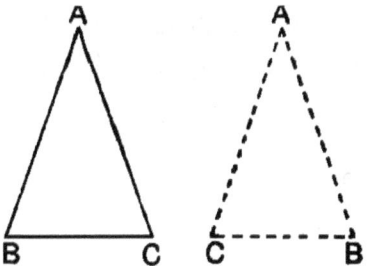

Now state the conclusion you draw from these experiments.

Lastly bisect the angle **BAC**, in your tracing, and fold the figure about the bisector. How does this experiment support your conclusion?

Exercise 6. Take the scalene triangle you have drawn in Exercise 2 (iii). Measure the angles. Which is the greatest side, and which is the greatest angle? Which is the smallest side, and which is the smallest angle?

Draw a triangle of any size and shape you like (not from measurements). Now measure the sides and angles. Write down the sides *a, b, c* in order of their lengths, beginning with the longest. Write down the angles **A**, **B**, **C** in order of their size, beginning with the largest.

State in your own words the conclusion you draw.

(i) In each of the six possible triangles given in Exercise 2 you have measured the angles; let us in each case add the three angles together, and write down the result thus:

A + B + C =   degrees.

Range the totals in a column; compare them carefully, always bearing in mind that there may be small errors in your measurements. Take the average.

(ii) Now draw any three triangles varying in size and shape (not from given measurements). Measure the angles in each case, and add them together. Compare the *sums*.

(iii) Draw a good sized triangle of any shape you like. Cut it out and tear off the corners. Fit these together at a point **O**; and observe the two outer straight edges. Do these fall in a straight line? If so, what do you learn from this experiment?

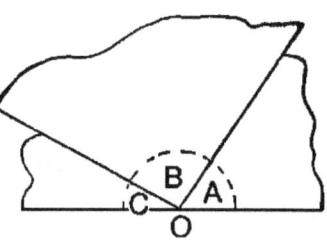

You have now reason for believing that in *any* triangle **ABC**

A + B + C = 180°;

or, in words, *the sum of the three angles is equal to* **two right angles**.

A triangle is said to be **right-angled** when *one* of its angles is a right angle.

Exercise 7. Draw a right-angled triangle. Can a triangle have more than one right angle? Can a right-angled triangle also have an obtuse angle? How many acute angles has a right-angled triangle?

A triangle is said to be **obtuse-angled** when *one* of its angles is obtuse.

TRIANGLES

Exercise 8. Draw an obtuse-angled triangle. How many acute angles must every obtuse-angled triangle have?

A triangle is **acute-angled** when *all three* of its angles are acute.

Exercise 9. Draw an acute-angled triangle. Why would it not be enough to say "A triangle is acute-angled when *one* of its angles is acute?"

Before constructing a triangle or other figure having given sides and angles, it is very useful to draw a rough free-hand sketch, in order to make sure that the question is understood, and to show what is given and what is required.

PROBLEM 12

To draw a triangle having given **two sides** *and the* **included angle.** (For instance: $b = 1.8''$, $c = 2.7''$, **A** $= 65°$.)

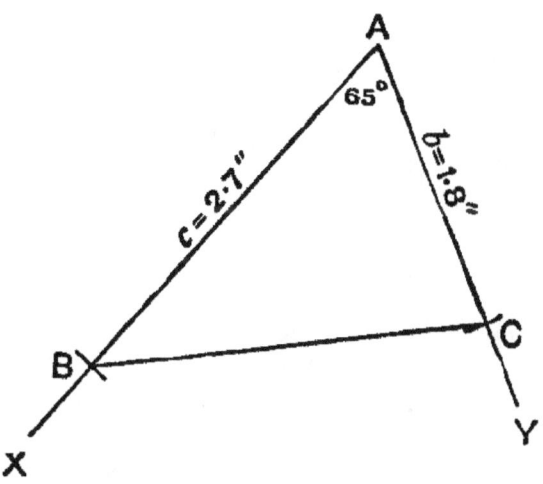

Construction. Draw a line **AX**; and from **A** draw **AY** making an angle of 65° with **AX** (using protractor).

From **AX** cut off **AB** equal to 2.7" (the length of c).

From **AY** cut off **AC** equal to 1.8" (the length of b).

Join **BC**.

Then **ABC** is evidently the required triangle.

[Measure the ∠^{s} at **B** and **C**,
and verify **A** + **B** + **C** = 180°.]

Exercise 10. Draw a right angle **BAC** (with protractor or set square), making **AB** and **AC** each 2.5″. Join **BC**.

Why are the angles at **B** and **C** equal? How many degrees are there in each?

Exercise 11. Draw a triangle in which b = 7.8 cm., c = 6.2 cm., and **A** = 118°. Measure a, **B**, and **C**; and verify **A** + **B** + **C** = 180°.

Exercise 12. Draw an isosceles triangle **ABC**, in which

AB = **AC** = 7.0 cm., and **A** = 84°.

Can you tell without measurement how many degrees there must be in each of the angles at **B** and **C**?

PROBLEM 13

To draw a triangle having given **one side** *and the* **two angles** *at its ends.* (For instance: a = 3.2″, **B** = 72°, **C** = 37°.)

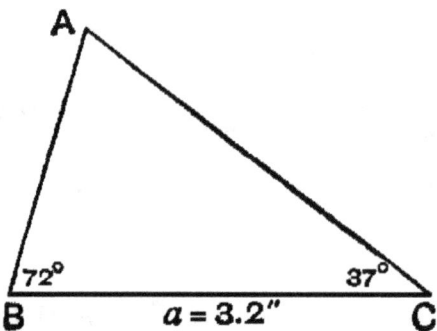

Construction. Draw **BC** equal to 3.2″.

At **B** make an angle of 72° with **BC** (using protractor).

At **C** make an angle of 37° with **CB**, on the same side as before.

TRIANGLES

Produce (that is to say, *prolong*) the lines to meet at **A**. Then **ABC** is the required triangle.

[State, without measuring, the size of the angle **A**: then test your answer with the protractor.]

(Comparison of Angles and Sides)

Exercise 13. Draw a triangle **ABC** in which $a = 6.8$ cm., **B** $= 101°$, and **C** $= 44°$. Say, before drawing, what must be the size of the angle **A**. Verify afterwards by measurement.

Exercise 14. Each of the angles at the base of a triangle is $65°$; what is the vertical angle?

Draw a triangle **ABC** in which $a = 2.4''$, **B** $=$ **C** $= 65°$. Measure b and c, and say what kind of triangle it is (i) in respect of its sides (ii) in respect of its angles.

Exercise 15. Draw a triangle **ABC** in which $b = 6.2$ cm., **A** $= 61°$, and **C** $= 35°$. What is the angle **B**? Measure a and c.

Write down (i) the sides, (ii) the angles in order of their size, and compare the two results.

Exercise 16. Try to draw triangles in which

(i) $a = 5.8$ cm., **B** $= 110°$, **C** $= 70°$;

(ii) $a = 5.8$ cm., **B** $= 45°$, **C** $= 135°$.

What difficulty arises? Perhaps you find that the other sides would not meet on your paper: would they *ever* meet? Give a reason for your answer.

Exercise 17. In a right-angled triangle, if one acute angle is $60°$, what is the other?

Draw a triangle in which $a = 3.0''$, **A** $= 90°$, **B** $= 60°$.

CHAPTER X

TRIANGLES CONTINUED: CONGRUENCE AND PRACTICAL APPLICATIONS

If you look back at Problems 11, 12, and 13, on the construction of triangles, you will notice that in each case *three* things were given: namely

(i) Three sides. (Problem 11);

(ii) Two sides and the included angle. (Problem 12);

(iii) One side and two angles. (Problem 13);

And these *data* (or things given) were enough to fix the size and shape of the triangle.

Exercise 1. Draw a good-sized triangle **ABC** of any shape; then state three different methods (corresponding to Problems 11, 12, and 13) by which an exact copy of it may be made.

Make a copy of the given triangle **ABC** in each of these ways; and test by seeing if a tracing of the triangle **ABC** can be exactly fitted over each copy.

Would the size and shape of a triangle be fixed if we were given the *three angles*? First of all, the sum of the three angles must be 180°, otherwise no triangle could be drawn from them.

Let us take **A** = 55°, **B** = 80°, **C** = 45°. Draw a line **BC** of *any* length as base. Make the angle **B** equal to 80°, and the angle **C** equal to 45°; then *whatever length we take for the base* **BC**, the third angle **A** must be 55°.

Thus any number of triangles of *different sizes* can be drawn having the given angles 55°, 80°, 45°. You will easily see that all these triangles have the *same shape*: in fact the three angles fix the *shape* but not the size of a triangle.

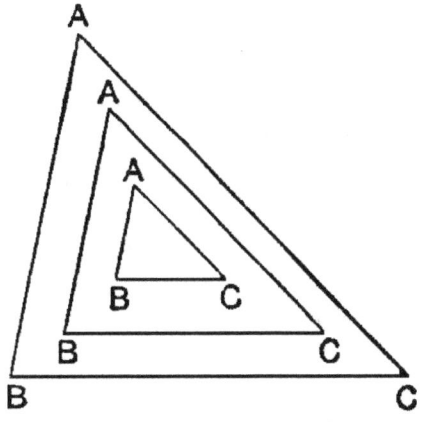

If a tracing of one triangle can be made to fit exactly over another, it is clear that the two triangles have the same size and shape, and are equal in all respects. The fitting of one figure over another for the purpose of comparison is called *superposition*; and if one figure *exactly* fits over the other, it is said to *coincide* with it. Figures which can be made to coincide with one another, thus showing that they have the same size and shape, are said to be *congruent*.

(Questions to be answered orally)

Exercise 2. In a △ **ABC**, **A** = 70°, **C** = 50°; what is **B**?

Exercise 3. In a △ **ABC**, **B** = 28°, **C** = 112°; what is **A**?

Exercise 4. How many triangles can there be in which **A** = 91°, **B** = 35°, **C** = 54°?

Exercise 5. How many triangles can there be in which **A** = 115°, **B** = 50°, **C** = 25°?

Exercise 6. A △ **ABC** is right-angled at **A**; if **B** = 55°, what is **C**?

Exercise 7. In a △ **ABC**, **B** = 65°, and **C** = 25°. What sort of triangle is it (i) in respect of its angles, (ii) in respect of its sides?

Exercise 8. The △ **ABC** is isosceles, **A** being the vertex. If **B** = 41°, what are the other angles?

Exercise 9. The △ **ABC** is isosceles, and the vertical angle **A** is 50°. What are the angles at **B** and **C**?

Exercise 10. The isosceles △ **ABC** is right-angled at the vertex **A**. What are the angles **B** and **C**?

Exercise 11. In a △ **ABC**, if **A** + **B** = **C**, what is the angle **C**?

(Exercises in Geometrical Drawing: The constructions to be done with ruler and compasses only unless otherwise stated)

Exercise 12. Draw a line **AB** of length 6 cm. Construct two equilateral triangles **APB**, **AQB** on opposite sides of **AB** as base.

Compare your construction with that of Problem 7 (p. 55), and explain why **PQ** bisects **AB** at right angles.

Exercise 13. On a base of 2.0" draw an isosceles triangle, each of the equal sides being 2.5".

From the vertex draw a perpendicular to the base; and show by measurement that this perpendicular bisects the vertical angle. Account for this by comparing the constructions of Problem 10 (p. 62) and Problem 3 (p. 41).

Exercise 14. Draw a triangle **ABC** in which $a = 7.6$ cm., **B** = 80°, **C** = 46°. (With protractor.)

Bisect the ∠ **BAC** (construction) by a line which meets the base at **X**. Calculate the ∠^{S} **AXB**, **AXC**; and verify by measurement.

Exercise 15. On a base **BC** of 8 cm. construct an isosceles triangle **ABC**, having the angle at each end of the base half a right angle. (With protractor.)

Bisect **BC** at right angles by a line **PQ**. Why does **PQ** pass through **A**?

Exercise 16. Construct a triangle, having given: $a = 5$ cm., **B** = 60°, **C** = 90°. (Without protractor.) What is the $\angle$ **A**?

Exercise 17. Construct an angle **BAC** of 120°. Make **AB** = **AC** = 7.2 cm. Join **BC**.

What are the angles at **B** and **C**? Measure **BC** to the nearest millimetre.

Exercise 18. Construct (with ruler and compasses only) a triangle **ABC**, having the two sides **AB**, **AC** equal to two given lines c and b, and the included angle **A** equal to a given angle **P**.

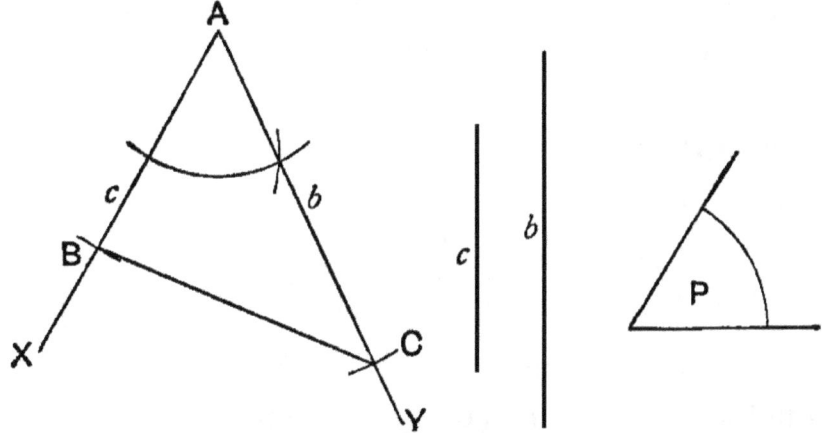

[This is Problem 12 set in a new form. We give the complete figure, and leave the details of construction to the pupil.]

Exercise 19. Construct (without protractor) a triangle **ABC**, having the side **BC** equal to the line a, and the angles **B** and **C** equal to the given angles **P** and **Q**.

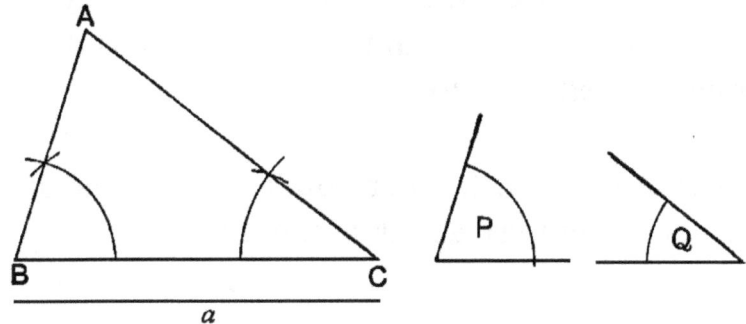

Exercise 20. Draw a straight line **PQ** of any length, and take a point **O** in it. From **O** draw two lines on the same side of **PQ**, and call the angles so formed **A**, **B**, and **C**.

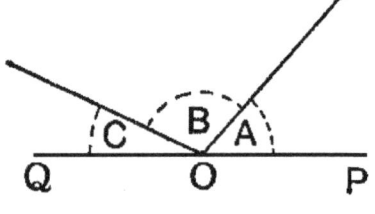

On a base of 3.4″ construct a triangle having the angles at each end of the base equal to **B** and **C**. How do you know that the third angle of this triangle must be equal to **A**?

Exercise 21. Draw a triangle **ABC** having sides 10 cm., 9 cm., 8 cm., in length.

Bisect each side at right angles (Problem 7). If your drawing is correct, the bisectors meet at a point. Call the meeting point **O**.

Measure the distances of **O** from **A**, **B**, and **C**. Can you account for these distances being the same?

From centre **O**, with radius **OA**, draw a circle: this should pass through **B** and **C**.

A circle which passes through all the vertices of a figure is said to be **circumscribed** about it.

Exercise 22. Construct a triangle in which $a = 2.7″$, $b = 3.0″$, and $c = 2.3″$; and draw a circle to pass through its vertices by the method of Exercise 21.

Exercise 23. Construct an equilateral triangle on a base of 7 cm., and circumscribe a circle about it.

TRIANGLES AND CONSTRUCTIONS

Exercise 24. Draw a good sized triangle of any shape. Through each vertex draw a line perpendicular to the opposite side (with set squares). What do you notice with regard to the meeting of the three perpendiculars?

Exercise 25. Draw a triangle of any shape. Bisect each of its angles by construction. If your drawing is correct, the bisectors meet at a point **O**.

From **O** draw a perpendicular (with set squares) to a side. With **O** as centre, and this perpendicular as radius, draw a circle. This circle should *touch* each of the three sides. It is said to be **inscribed** in the triangle.

(Practical Applications. Heights and Distances)

The following problems are to be solved by measuring diagrams carefully drawn to scale. Since however it is impossible either to draw or to measure with absolute accuracy, it follows that results so obtained can only be **approximate**; that is to say, they will be near enough to the truth to be of practical value, though they cannot be relied upon as strictly accurate. Careful work should usually yield a result within *one* per cent. of that given in the *Answers*.

The direction which we call **vertical** (or upright) is that taken by a thread from one end of which a weight hangs freely at rest. Any straight line at right angles to a vertical line is said to be **horizontal** (or *level*).

Exercise 26. How many vertical lines can be drawn through a given point? How many horizontal lines?

EXPERIMENTAL AND PRACTICAL GEOMETRY

In the diagram given below **P** represents some object whose height or distance is to be found, and **O** the position of the observer's eye; so that **OP** is the *line of sight*, that is, the direction in which the object is seen. Let **OP** be the *horizontal* line passing from the observer's eye directly *under* or *over* the object **P**.

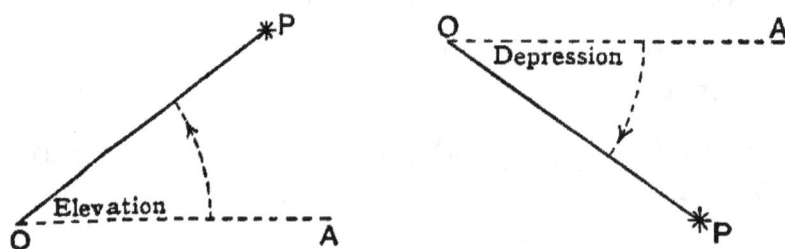

Then the ∠ **AOP** is called the **angle of elevation**, when the object is *above* the horizontal line; and the **angle of depression** when the object is *below* the horizontal line.

Exercise 27. On my estate there are two farms. One lies S.E. of my house, and 350 yards from it; the other lies S.W. of the house at a distance of 250 yards. How far are the farms apart? (Scale 100 yards to 1 inch.)

Exercise 28. Havre lies due West of Rouen, distant 72 kilometres. Dieppe lies due North of Rouen, distant 56 kilometres. How does Dieppe bear from Havre, and what is the distance between the two places? (Scale 10 km. to 1 cm.)

Exercise 29. A shore battery, whose guns have an effective range of 7000 yards (say 4 miles), fires on an enemy's ship bearing N.W. from the battery and distant 2½ miles. On this the ship steams N.E., 2 miles, then drops anchor, thinking herself out of range. Is she? (Scale 1 mile to 1 inch.)

Exercise 30. A tower is observed from a point on the ground 500 feet distant from its foot, and the angle of elevation of the top is found to be 15°. What is the height of the tower? (Scale 100 feet to 1 inch.)

TRIANGLES AND CONSTRUCTIONS

Exercise 31. A vertical pole, 21 feet high, is found to cast a shadow 35 feet long. How many degrees is the sun above the horizon? (Scale 10 feet to 1 inch.)

Exercise 32. From a point **A** I walk 200 yards due West: I then turn N.E., and walk till I get to a point **C** from which **A** appears due South. Then I return straight to **A**. How far have I walked altogether? (Scale 100 yards to 1 inch.)

Exercise 33. A balloon, held captive by a rope 200 metres long, has drifted in the wind till its angle of elevation, as observed from the place of ascent, is 54°. How high is the balloon above the ground? (Scale 20 metres to 1 cm.)

Exercise 34. From a vessel's fore-top, 80 feet above the sea, a buoy is observed, and the angle of depression found to be 9°. How far is the buoy from the ship? (Scale 100 feet to 1 inch.)

Exercise 35. In surveying an estate I note three cottages **A**, **B**, and **C**. I walk from **A** due East to **B**, the distance being 350 metres, and **C** is on my left hand. The distance from **A** to **C** is 120 metres, and from **B** to **C** 370 metres. In what direction does **C** bear from **A**? (Scale 100 metres to 2 cm.)

Exercise 36. A triangular field is enclosed by two hedges and a ditch. The hedges are each 150 yards long, and they make an angle of 64°. Draw a plan (scale 50 yards to 1 inch), and find the length of the ditch.

Exercise 37. From Dover the bearing of Calais is E. 31° S.; that of Boulogne is E. 63° S.; and the distances of the two French ports from Dover are respectively 23 miles and 31 miles. How far is Boulogne from Calais? (Scale 10 miles to 1 inch.)

Exercise 38. A straight canal runs through my grounds, and is bridged at two places 400 yards apart. The house is 250 yards from each bridge. How far is it from the house to the nearest point on the canal? (Choose a suitable scale for yourself.)

EXPERIMENTAL AND PRACTICAL GEOMETRY

Exercise 39. Two ships **A** and **B** drop anchor, 2 cable's lengths apart, **B** bearing N.W. from **A**. A signal station ashore bears N.E. from **A** and due E. from **B**. How far is each ship from the signal station? [N.B. 1 cable = 200 yards.]

Exercise 40. There are three towns **A**, **B**, and **C**. Of these, **B** is East of **A**, and distant 35 miles; while **C** is North of **A**, and distant 84 miles. A straight railway connects **B** and **C**. How far is **A** from the nearest point on this railway? (Scale 10 miles to 1 cm.)

Exercise 41. From a certain point on the ground I observe the top of a spire, and find the angle of elevation to be 33°. I advance 80 feet towards the spire, and then find the angle of elevation to be 47°. How high is the spire? (Scale 40 ft. to 1 inch.)

Exercise 42. A man, standing 15 feet away from the base of a monument, finds that the angle of elevation of the summit is 45°; and in making the observation his eye is 5 feet above the level of the ground. Find the height of the monument. (Scale 5 feet to 1 inch.)

Exercise 43. If a man, whose height is 6 feet, stands 12 feet from a certain lamp-post, he finds that his shadow cast by the light is 12 feet in length. How high is the light above the ground?

Exercise 44. From a point on a plain I observe a beacon which stands on the summit of a neighbouring hill, and I find its angle of elevation to be 14°. I walk 700 metres over the plain towards the hill, and then find the angle of elevation to be 31°. How high is the beacon above the level of the plain?

CHAPTER XI
QUADRILATERALS

Any figure bounded by four straight sides is called a **quadrilateral**.

Before attempting to draw a quadrilateral from given sides and angles be sure to make a rough preliminary freehand sketch, writing in the given dimensions. This will show you clearly what is given and what is required. In this Section, set squares are to be used for drawing parallels and perpendiculars unless otherwise stated.

Draw two lines making at **A** an angle of 68°. Along one arm mark off **AB** equal to 2.5"; and along the other mark off **AD** equal to 2.0".

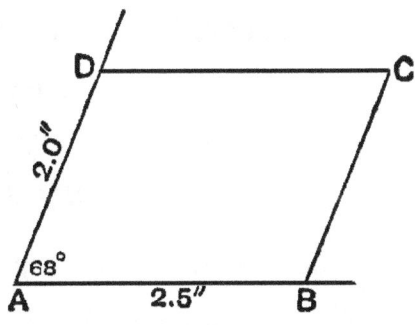

Through **B** draw a line parallel to **AD**.

Through **D** draw a line parallel to **AB**, cutting the first parallel at **C**.

The four-sided figure you have thus drawn is a **parallelogram**.

A **parallelogram** is a quadrilateral *whose opposite sides are parallel*.

Measure **DC** and **BC**, and compare them with **AB** and **AD**.

EXPERIMENTAL AND PRACTICAL GEOMETRY

Can you tell from what you have learned of parallels how many degrees there are in the angles **ABC, ADC, BCD**? Test your answer by measurement.

Exercise 1. Draw a parallelogram **ABCD** from the following data: The $\angle$ **A** = 114°, **AB** = 7.5 cm., **AD** = 5.5 cm.

Measure **DC** and **BC**, and compare them with the given sides. Write down the number of degrees in each of the angles **ABC, ADC, BCD**; and test by measurement.

Exercise 2. Draw a parallelogram **ABCD** in which the $\angle$ **B** = 42°, **AB** = 8.2 cm. and **BC** = 6.4 cm.

Measure and compare (i) the opposite sides, (ii) the opposite angles; and write down the results you get.

Exercise 3. Draw a parallelogram **ABCD** in which the $\angle$ **A** is a *right angle*, **AB** = 2.8″, **AD** = 1.7″.

Measure **DC** and **BC**, and compare them with the given sides. What are the other angles of the figure, and why?

Exercise 4. Draw a parallelogram **ABCD** from the following data: The $\angle$ **A** = a *right angle*, and **AB** = **AD** = 6.5 cm.

Measure **DC** and **BC**: do you find all the sides equal?

What are the remaining angles of the figure, and why?

A parallelogram which has a right angle is called a **rectangle**.

A rectangle in which two sides forming a right angle are equal is called a **square**.

QUADRILATERALS

Exercise 5. Draw a parallelogram **ABCD**, in which the ∠ **A** = 122°, and **AB** = **AD** = 7 cm.

Measure **DC** and **BC**: do you find the sides all equal?

Write down the number of degrees in each of the angles **ABC, BCD, ADC**.

A **rhombus** is a parallelogram in which two sides which meet are equal, but it has no right angle.

Notice that the *rectangle*, the *square*, and the *rhombus* are all special forms of the parallelogram.

We will now gather together the conclusions that may be drawn from the foregoing exercises.

(i) In a parallelogram, what do you infer about the opposite sides? What about the opposite angles?

(ii) Are all the sides of a square equal? Why?

(iii) Are all the sides of a rhombus equal? Why?

(iv) If one angle of a parallelogram is a right angle, what can you tell about the other angles?

(v) What do you conclude about the angles of a *rectangle*? What about the angles of a *square*?

Each of the straight lines which join opposite vertices of a quadrilateral is called a **diagonal**.

Exercise 6. Draw an *oblique parallelogram* (that is, having no right angle), a *rectangle*, a *square*, and a *rhombus*. Call each figure **ABCD**. In each case draw the two diagonals, and let them cross at **O**. Now ascertain by measuring or other experiment to which of these four figures the following statements apply:

(i) *The diagonals bisect one another.*

(ii) *The diagonals cross at right angles.*

(iii) *The diagonals are equal.*

(iv) *Each diagonal divides the figure into two triangles of the same size and shape.* (Make a tracing of the △ **ABC**, and see if it can be exactly fitted over the △ **ADC**.)

(v) *The figure is symmetrical about a diagonal.* (That is, if the figure is folded about a diagonal, the two parts coincide.)

Exercise 7. About which of the four figures of Exercise 6 can a circle be circumscribed having its centre at **O**, and **OA** as radius?

Exercise 8. Using your protractor and set squares, draw a rhombus having each side 6.5 cm. in length, and one angle equal to 82°. Enter into your figure (without measurement) the values of the other angles.

Exercise 9. On a side of 2.5″ construct a square with ruler and compasses only. Measure each diagonal to the nearest tenth of an inch.

Exercise 10. Draw a line **AC**, 3″ long. With ruler and compasses only construct a square having **AC** as diagonal; and measure its sides.

[First step of construction: Bisect **AC** at right angles.]

Exercise 11. Construct a rhombus whose diagonals are 8 cm. and 6 cm. (using ruler and compasses). Measure each side.

Exercise 12. Draw a parallelogram **ABCD**, in which the sides **AB**, **AD** are 6.5 cm. and 5.5 cm., and the diagonal **BD** is 9 cm.

[Construct the △ **ABD** (Problem 11); then complete the parallelogram with set squares.]

QUADRILATERALS

PROBLEM 14

To construct a quadrilateral **ABCD**, *having the angle at* **A** *equal to a given angle* **P**, *and the sides of given lengths.* (For instance: **AB** = 8 cm., **BC** = 5 cm., **CD** = 6 cm., **DA** = 7 cm.)

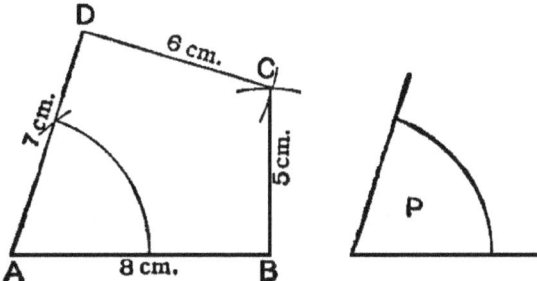

Construction. Construct an angle at **A** equal to the given angle **P**; and from its arms cut off **AB** equal to 8 cm., and **AD** equal to 7 cm.

With centre **D**, and radius 6 cm., draw an arc.

With centre **B**, and radius 5 cm., cut the first arc at **C**.

Join **BC, DC**.

Then **ABCD** is the required quadrilateral.

NOTE. If the ∠ **A** is given in *degrees*, it must be made with the protractor.

Exercise 13. Draw quadrilaterals from the rough plans given below; the dimensions are to be in centimetres.

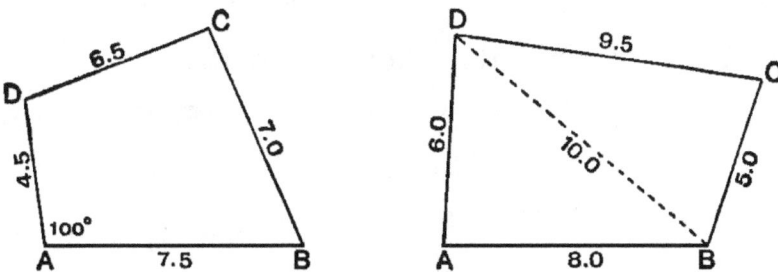

[In the right-hand figure first construct the △ **ABD** (Problem 11), then proceed as above.]

EXPERIMENTAL AND PRACTICAL GEOMETRY

Exercise 14. In a quadrilateral **ABCD**,

AB = 3.5″, **BC** = 3.0″, **CD** = 2.5″, **DA** = 2.0″.

Show that the *shape* of the figure is not fixed by these data.

Draw the quadrilateral from the above dimensions, when

(i) **A** = 60°;   (ii) **A** = 90°.

How many things must be given in order to fix the size and shape of a quadrilateral?

Exercise 15. In surveying a quadrilateral field **ABCD**, I go from **A** to **B** due East, and find that **AB** = 50 metres; from **B** to **C** North East, and **BC** = 60 metres; from **C** to **D** due West, and **CD** = 135 metres.

Plot the field, (scale 10 metres to 1 cm.). Measure **DA** on your plan: what is the real length of this side? How does **D** bear from **A**? Show by any test you like that the sides **AB**, **CD** are parallel.

A quadrilateral that has *one* pair of parallel sides is called a **trapezium**.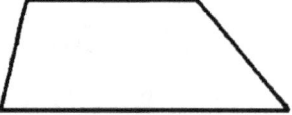

Exercise 16. Draw a parallelogram whose diagonals are 8 cm. and 6 cm. in length, and intersect one another at an angle of 54°. Find by measurement the length of the perimeter.

Exercise 17. I want a plan of a quadrilateral field **ABCD**, and I have with me no means of measuring *angles*.

I therefore measure the following lengths:

AB = 350 yards,   **AC** = 300 yards,   **BC** = 200 yards;
AD = 230 yards,   **BD** = 350 yards.

QUADRILATERALS

Plot the field from these dimensions, and measure the side **CD**.

[First construct the △ **ABC** (Problem 11), scale 100 yards to 1 in.; then construct the △ **ABD**. Finally join **CD**.]

Exercise 18. Draw a good sized quadrilateral **ABCD** of any shape; and make an exact copy of it by each of the following constructions:

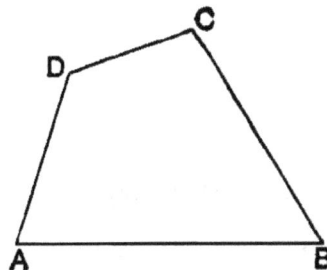 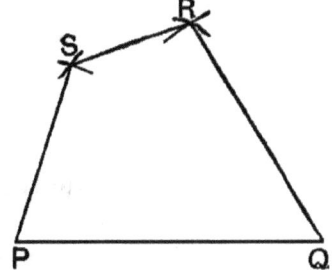

Draw **PQ** equal to **AB**.

(i) Make the ∠ **P** equal to the ∠ **A** (with your protractor, if this is allowed; otherwise by construction). Cut off **PS** equal to **AD**.

Make the ∠ **PQR** equal to the ∠ **B**; and cut off **QR** equal to **BC**.

Join **SR**.

(ii) With centre **P**, and radius equal to **AD**, draw an arc.

With centre **Q**, and radius equal to **BD**, cut the first arc at **S**.

With centre **P**, and radius equal to **AC**, draw an arc.

With centre **Q**, and radius equal to **BC**, cut the last arc at **R**.

Join **SR**.

NOTE. A figure of *five*, or more, sides may be reproduced by similar constructions.

EXPERIMENTAL AND PRACTICAL GEOMETRY

Exercise 19. Draw the patterns shown below:

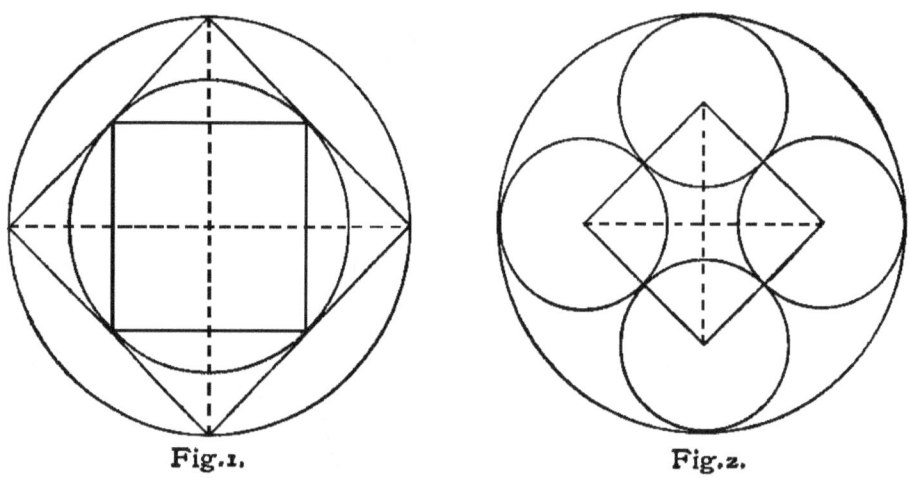

Fig. 1.   Fig. 2.

Figure 1. First draw the larger square from diagonals of 3″.

Figure 2. First draw the square from diagonals of 2″; then the small circles; finally the outside circle.

CHAPTER XII

AREAS

In the squared paper used in this Section the horizontal lines are *one-tenth* of an inch apart, and the perpendicular lines are also *one-tenth* of an inch apart; so that the whole surface of the paper is divided into little squares, each on a side of one-tenth of an inch.

The figure **ABCD** is a rectangle whose length **AB** is 1.5″, and whose breadth **AD** is 0.8″; so that the length and breadth contain respectively 15 and 8 *tenths of an inch*.

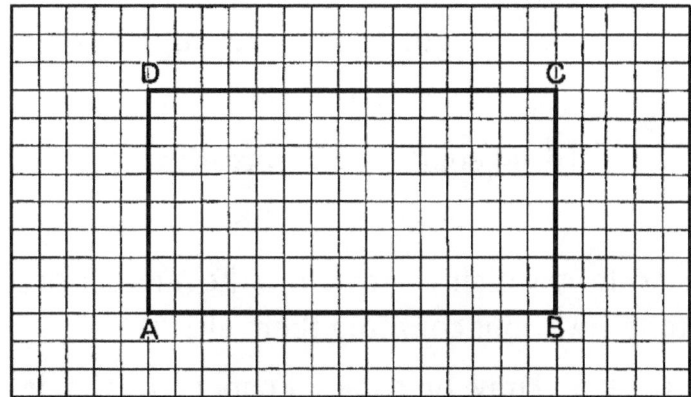

Drawing not to scale

Now let us reckon the number of squares that fall within this rectangle.

These squares lie in *rows* parallel to **AB**. How many squares are there in each row? How many rows are there? How many squares then are there altogether in the rectangle?

Again the squares stand in *columns* parallel to **AD**. How many squares are there in each column? How many columns? How many squares altogether?

The total number of squares within the rectangle gives you an idea of the **area**, that is to say, the *amount of space* enclosed within its boundaries.

Exercise 1. Draw on squared paper a rectangle whose length is 2.0″, or 20 *tenths* of an inch, and whose breadth is 0.9″, or 9 *tenths*.

Count the number of squares in each row, and the number of rows. How many squares are there in the rectangle?

Check your answer by counting the number of squares in each column, and the number of columns.

Exercise 2. Draw the following rectangles on squared paper, and find their areas (measured in squares on one-tenth of an inch):

(i) Length = 2.0″, breadth = 1.0″;

(ii) Length = 1.5″, breadth = 1.2″;

(iii) Length = 2.5″, breadth = 0.8″;

(iv) Length = 1.6″, breadth = 0.5″.

State a rule by which you can find the number of squares in each rectangle without counting them all.

Exercise 3. Draw on squared paper a rectangle of length 1.2″, making the breadth such that the rectangle will contain 84 ruled squares.

Exercise 4. Consider the figures given on the opposite page. Which do you think contains the greatest area? Which the least?

Now count the squares in each figure, and see if your guess is correct.

AREAS

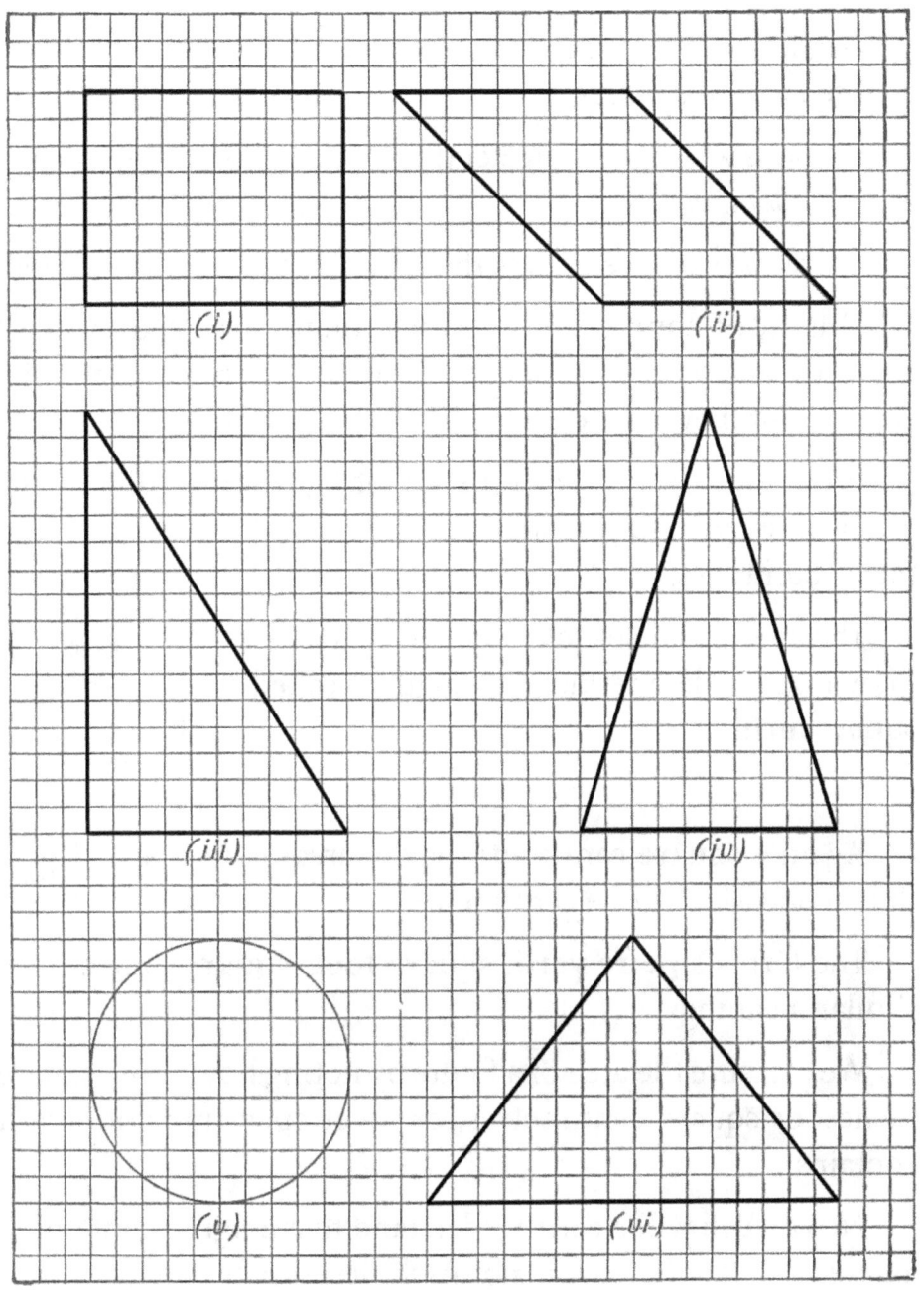

Drawing not to scale

[In several of these figures the outlines run *through* some of the squares. In such cases

portions of a square which seem to be one-half should be counted as *half-squares*;

portions which seem greater than one-half should be counted as *whole squares*;

portions which seem less than one-half should be omitted.

This is, of course, a somewhat rough and ready way of counting, and results so obtained cannot be expected to be quite correct; but they will be near enough for our present purpose.]

From these examples you see that figures may differ completely in shape, and yet *contain the same amount of space* within their boundaries.

The amount of space contained in a square drawn on a side one inch in length is called a **square inch**.

Again a **square centimetre** is the area of a square drawn on a side of one centimetre.

The terms **square yard**, **square foot**, **square metre** have similar meanings.

We measure the area of a figure by noting how many square inches, or square centimetres, or other such units of area it contains.

NOTE. You will clearly understand that a figure containing an area of 1 *square inch* is not itself necessarily square: it may be triangular, or circular, or of any other shape, provided that its boundaries enclose exactly as much space as that contained within a square on a side of 1 inch.

AREAS

(Areas of squares and rectangles)

Exercise 5. Draw on squared paper a square on a side of 1 inch. How many squares does it contain, each on a side of *one-tenth* of an inch?

Exercise 6. Draw two straight lines, one double the length of the other; and on each draw a square. How many times does the greater square contain the less? Draw lines in the greater square to illustrate your answer.

Exercise 7. Draw on squared paper a rectangle 1.5″ long by 1.0″ wide.

(i) If you treble the length, without altering the width, how many times do you multiply the area?

(ii) If you treble both length and breadth, how many times do you multiply the area?

(iii) If you treble the length, and double the breadth, how many times do you multiply the area?

In each case draw a figure to illustrate your answer.

Exercise 8. Draw a line **AB**, 3″ long. Suppose each inch to stand for 1 foot, so that the whole line represents 1 yard.

Draw a square on **AB**: then this square represents 1 *square yard*. In the corner of this figure draw a square to represent 1 square foot.

Now show why 1 square yard = 9 square feet.

Exercise 9. A passage is 20 feet long by 10 feet wide. Draw a plan of the floor on squared paper (scale 10 feet to 1 inch).

How is a square foot represented on your plan'? Find the area of the floor in square feet.

EXPERIMENTAL AND PRACTICAL GEOMETRY

Exercise 10. A court-yard is 25 yards long by 15 yards wide. Draw a plan on squared paper (scale 10 yards to 1 inch).

What area is represented by one of the ruled squares of your paper? Find the area of the court-yard.

Exercise 11. Find the area of the rectangles of which the length and breadth are given below.

The areas are to be got by calculation; but it will be a useful exercise to draw a plan on squared paper in each case. Choose your own scale.

(i) Length = 18 in., breadth = 10 in.; Ans. in sq. in.
(ii) Length = 25 ft., breadth = 16 ft.; Ans. in sq. ft.
(iii) Length = 45 metres, breadth = 22 metres; Ans. in sq. m.
(iv) Length = 2 ft. 1 in., breadth = 8 in.; Ans. in sq. in.
(v) Length = 5 ft., breadth = 48 in.; Ans. in sq. ft.

Exercise 12. The area of a rectangle is 6 square inches, and its length is 3 inches. What is its breadth? Draw the rectangle.

Exercise 13. Draw a rectangle 5 cm. long, and of sufficient breadth to give the figure an area of 20 sq. cm.

Exercise 14. What is the breadth of a rectangle, if its area is 4 sq. in., and its length is 2½″? Draw the rectangle on squared paper, and thus verify your work.

Exercise 15. If in a plan 1 inch represents 8 feet, what does 1 *square inch* represent?

Exercise 16. In the plan of a quadrangle 1 inch stands for 10 feet: what is represented by 1 *square inch*?

If the length of the plan is 5″, and the breadth is 4″, what is the area of the quadrangle?

Exercise 17. Find the area of a rectangular pavement, of which a plan, scale 5 feet to 1 in., measures 8″ long by 6″ wide.

Exercise 18. In a certain map 1″ represents 5 miles: what area is represented by a rectangle 2.5″ long by 2.0″ wide?

Exercise 19. If 100 yards of railing are required to fence in a square paddock, what is its area?

Exercise 20. The length of a rectangular field is 50 yards: the total distance round it is 180 yards. What is the breadth? Find the area.

(Area of a parallelogram)

Drawing not to scale

We wish to ascertain the area of the parallelogram **ABCD**, and in particular to compare it with that of the rectangle **ABEF** on the same base **AB** and of the same height **BE**.

(i) Count the number of ruled squares in the parallelogram, as explained on p. 94.

Then measure the length **AB** and the height **BE** in tenths of an inch. Multiply together the number of tenths in the length and height. The product gives you the number of ruled squares in the rectangle **ABEF**.

Do you get the same, or nearly the same, result for the parallelogram and rectangle? (Remember that your system of counting in the first case is not likely to give a quite correct answer.)

(ii) Make a careful copy of the parallelogram **ABCD**, and cut it out from your paper. Next rule the line **BE**; and, cutting along it, remove the triangle **BEC**.

Now place the triangle **BEC** on the other side of the remaining figure **ABED**, so that **BC** fits along **AD**.

You see that by thus changing the position of the triangle **BEC** you have converted the parallelogram into a rectangle.

We conclude that *in this case* the area of the parallelogram is equal to that of the rectangle on the same base and of the same height.

This we may express by saying, that

the area of a parallelogram = base **x** *height.*

[For a general and formal proof of this, see *School Geometry*, pp. 104, 105.]

Exercise 21. Draw on squared paper any oblique parallelogram whose base measures 15, and height 8 tenths of an inch.

Draw a rectangle of equal area; and test your work by counting the number of ruled squares in each figure.

Exercise 22. Draw any oblique parallelogram having a base of 3.0″, and height of 2.0″; then draw a rectangle of equal area.

How many such parallelograms could be drawn? How can we tell that they must all have the same area?

Exercise 23. Draw a parallelogram **ABCD**, in which the length = 8 cm., the height = 5 cm., and the $\angle$ A = 45° (with protractor).

Cut your figure out, and by dissection convert it into a rectangle of the same base and height.

Exercise 24. Rule on your squared paper a rectangle of length 2.5″ and breadth 2.0″.

On the same base draw a parallelogram having the same height as the rectangle, and one angle equal to 60°. (Use your protractor.)

Find the area of each figure.

Exercise 25. Given a square on a side of 6 cm., draw a parallelogram of equal area on the same base, having an angle of 75°.

What is the area of each figure?

Exercise 26. On a base of 2.0″ draw a rhombus having an angle of 50°; and on the same base draw a rectangle of equal area.

Measure the breadth of the rectangle, and hence calculate the area of each figure.

Exercise 27. Give a construction for drawing a parallelogram **ABCD**, having two adjacent sides **AB**, **AD** equal to 7 cm. and 6 cm. respectively, and having a height of 4 cm. Find its area.

Exercise 28. Draw a parallelogram **ABCD**, in which **AB** = 8 cm., **AD** = 6 cm., and the $\angle$ **A** = 72°.

Measure the height of the figure, and hence calculate its area.

EXPERIMENTAL AND PRACTICAL GEOMETRY

(Area of a triangle)

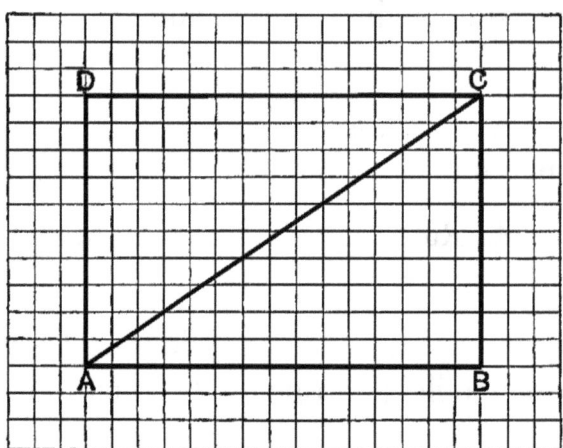

Drawing not to scale

In the rectangle **ABCD** we have drawn the diagonal **AC**, thus dividing the figure into two *right-angled* triangles.

We have already found (Exercise 6, p. 86) that these triangles are equal in all respects, so that the area of each is half that of the triangle.

This being so, we can find the number of ruled squares in the triangle **ABC** by calculating the number in the rectangle **ABCD**, and then taking half the result. Test this by counting the squares in the triangle **ABC**.

In the next figure the triangle **ABC** is not right-angled; but **BCDE** is still the rectangle on the same base **BC** and of the same height **AF**.

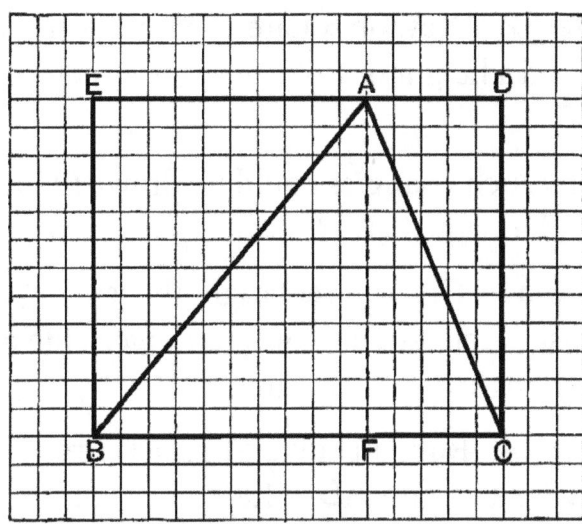

Drawing not to scale

Now the △ **AFB** is half the rectangle **AFBE**; why?

And the △ **AFC** is half the rectangle **AFCD**; why?

Hence if we add these areas together, we see that the △ **ABC** is half the rectangle **BCDE**.

That is to say,

area of △ **ABC** = ½ (base **BC** x height **AF**).

Exercise 29. Draw on squared paper a right-angled triangle **ABC**, making the right angle at **B**; and make **BC** = 3.0″, and **BA** = 2.0″.

Now complete the rectangle **ABCD**. What is its area? What is the area of the triangle **ABC**?

Exercise 30. On your squared paper rule a square on a side of 2.0″. Draw a right-angled triangle of half the area.

Test your work by counting the ruled squares.

EXPERIMENTAL AND PRACTICAL GEOMETRY

Exercise 31. On a base of 8.0 cm. draw a triangle of height 5.0 cm.; then draw a rectangle of double the area.

What is the area of the triangle in square centimetres?

Exercise 32. Draw on squared paper *any* triangle having a base of 2.5″ and a height of 1.6″; and rule a rectangle of double the area.

How many such triangles could be drawn? How can we tell that they are all of equal area?

Exercise 33. Given a rectangle measuring 2.8″ by 1.5″ (rule this on squared paper): on the longer side as base draw an isosceles triangle of half the area.

Exercise 34. Rule on squared paper a rectangle **ABCD**, in which **AB** = 3.0″, and **AD** = 1.8″.

On the base **AB** draw two triangles **APB, AQB**, each having half the area of the rectangle:

in (i) **AP** is to be 2.6″ in length (by compass construction);
in (ii) the ∠ **QAB** is to be 42° (use protractor).

Exercise 35. One side of a triangular field measures 120 yards, and the shortest distance between the opposite corner and this side is 80 yards. Find the area of the field in square yards.

Exercise 36. There are two plots of ground, one triangular and the other square.

The largest side of the triangular plot is 96 metres, and the perpendicular on it from the opposite corner is 27 metres.

Each side of the square plot measures 36 metres. Which plot has the larger area?

AREAS

Exercise 37. Draw an equilateral triangle **ABC** on a base of 2.0″.

Drop a perpendicular **AD** from the vertex **A** on the base **BC**. Measure **AD** as accurately as you can.

Now find approximately the area of the triangle in square inches.

Exercise 38. Construct a triangle **ABC**, having given $a = 8$ cm., $b = 7$ cm., $c = 6$ cm.

Draw and measure the perpendicular from **A** on **BC**, and hence calculate the approximate area of the triangle.

Exercise 39. Draw a triangle **ABC** from the following data:

$$a = 7.2 \text{ cm.}, \quad \mathbf{B} = 68°, \quad \mathbf{C} = 54°.$$

Draw and measure the perpendicular from **A** on **BC**, and hence reckon the approximate area of the triangle.

Exercise 40. (i) Draw an oblique parallelogram, a rectangle, and a triangle, all on the same base and of the same height.

How can you show from this figure that the area of the triangle is half that of the parallelogram?

(ii) Draw any triangle **ABC** (not isosceles) on a given base **BC**. Bisect the base at **X**, and join **AX**.

How can you tell that the two triangles **ABX**, **ACX**, though of different shape, have the same area?

CHAPTER XIII

MISCELLANEOUS CONSTRUCTIONS, CIRCLES, REGULAR POLYGONS

PROBLEM 15

Given the circumference of a circle, to find its centre.

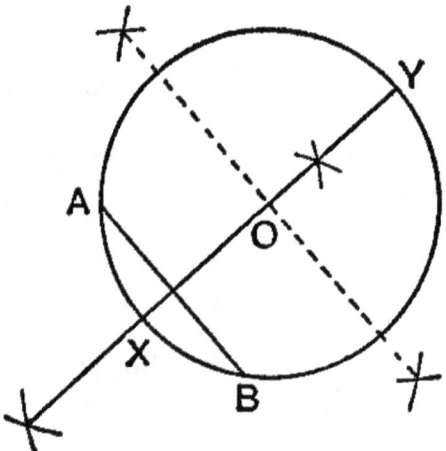

Construction. Draw any chord **AB**.

Bisect **AB** at right angles (Problem 7, p. 55) by a line which cuts the circumference at **X** and **Y**.

Bisect **XY** at **O**. Then **O** is the centre.

(Verification)

In Exercise 5, p. 57 you found several points whose distances from two given points **A** and **B** were equal; and on comparison, it appeared that all such points lay on a certain line: what line?

Now the centre is a point whose distances from **A** and **B** are equal; so the centre lies on that same line. Thus we have been able to draw a diameter **XY**; and by bisecting this, to find the centre.

(The Angle in a Semi-circle)

Draw a good sized semi-circle, say of radius 6 cm., and call its diameter **AB**. On the semi-circumference take three or four points **P, Q, R, ...**; and join each of them to **A** and **B**.

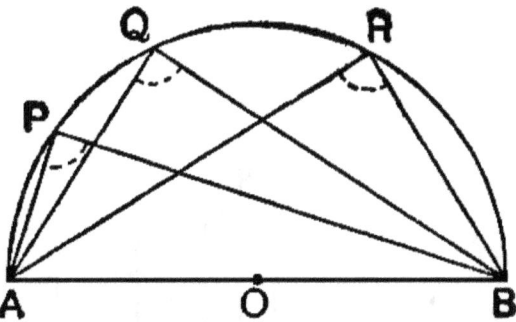

Now measure the angles **APB, AQB, ARB**; and enter the results in your figure.

Repeat this experiment with another semi-circle of any size you please, and again record your results.

You have now, no doubt, found in the instances you have examined, that if you join a point on the semi-circumference to the ends of the diameter, the angle so formed is *a right-angle*.

This result we express by saying that the *angle in a semi-circle is a right angle*.

Several important constructions follow from this property of a semi-circle.

Exercise 1. *Draw a straight line perpendicular to a given straight line **AB** from a given point **X** outside it,* **X** BEING NEARLY OPPOSITE ONE END OF **AB**.

[In this case the construction of Problem 10, p. 62 is inconvenient, and in its place we may use the following.]

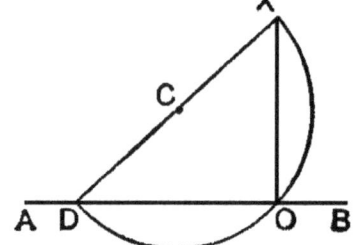

Construction. Take any point **D** in **AB**. Join **DX**; and bisect **DX** at **C**.

On **DX** draw a semi-circle to cut **AB** at **O**.

Join **XO**, and explain why it is perpendicular to **AB**.

(Tangents to a Circle)

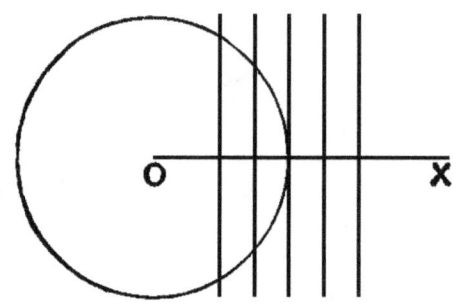

With any point **O** as centre, and a radius of 4 cm., draw a circle. Draw a radius, and produce it to **X**.

In **OX** take points at distances of 2 cm., 3 cm., 4 cm., 5 cm., and 6 cm. from **O**.

Through these points draw lines with your set squares perpendicular to **OX**.

Notice if, and how, these perpendiculars meet the circumference.

If the distance of the perpendicular from the centre is *less than the radius*, in how many points does the perpmdicular meet the circle? If greater, in how many points? If equal to the radius, in how many points?

CIRCLES, POLYGONS

From this and similar experiments you may learn that a line drawn perpendicular to a radius through its extremity meets the circumference at *one point only*. Such a line is said to *touch* the circle at that point, and is called a **tangent**.

Observe that only *one* tangent can be drawn to a circle at a given point on its circumference. Why so?

Exercise 2. In a circle of radius 1.8″ draw a diameter **AB**. Then with your set squares draw tangents at **A** and **B**, and show that these are parallel.

Exercise 3. Draw a straight line **AB** and take a point **X** in it. If a circle touches **AB** at **X**, on what line must its centre lie?

Draw two circles of radius 3.0 cm. to touch **AB** on opposite sides at the point **X**.

Exercise 4. Draw two concentric circles of radius 6.0 cm. and 6.5 cm. Draw a chord of the larger circle to touch the smaller, and measure its length.

PROBLEM 16

To draw a pair of tangents to a circle from a given point **T** *outside it.*

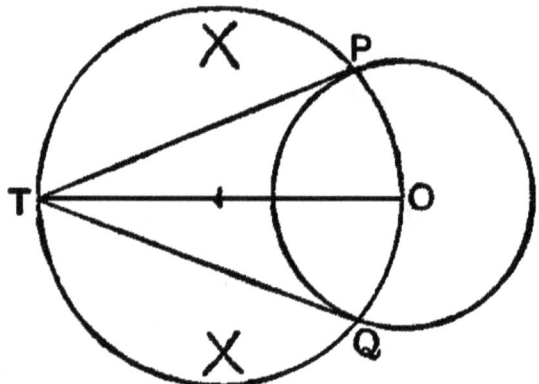

Construction. Join **T** to **O** the centre of the given circle, and bisect **TO**.

On **TO** as diameter draw a circle cutting the given circle at **P** and **Q**.

Draw **TP** and **TQ**, which are the required tangents.

(Verification)

Draw the radius **OP**. Then if the ∠ **OPT** is a right angle, **PT** is a tangent. Now the ∠ **OPT** is an angle in a semi-circle, and therefore a right angle.

Exercise 5. Draw a circle of radius 1.5″, and from a point 2.5″ distant from the centre draw a pair of tangents to the circle.

Measure the lengths of the tangents, and note that they are equal.

Exercise 6. Draw a circle of radius 4.0 cm. Take any two points **P** and **Q**, each at a distance of 10.4 cm. from the centre. From **P** and **Q** draw pairs of tangents to the circle.

Show by measurement that all four tangents are equal.

Exercise 7. Take two points **A** and **B**, 3 cm. apart. With **A** and **B** as centres, and a radius of 3 cm., draw circles. Produce **AB** both ways to cut the first circle at **X** and the other at **Y**.

From **X** draw a pair of tangents to the circle whose centre is **B**.

From **Y** draw a pair of tangents to the circle whose centre is **A**.

What sort of quadrilateral is the figure so formed?

A figure bounded by more than four sides is called a **polygon**. It is said to be **regular** if all its sides are equal, and all its angles are equal.

The most important regular polygons are these:

A **pentagon**, which has *five* sides; a **hexagon**, *six* sides;

an **octagon**, which has *eight* sides;   a **decagon**, *ten* sides.

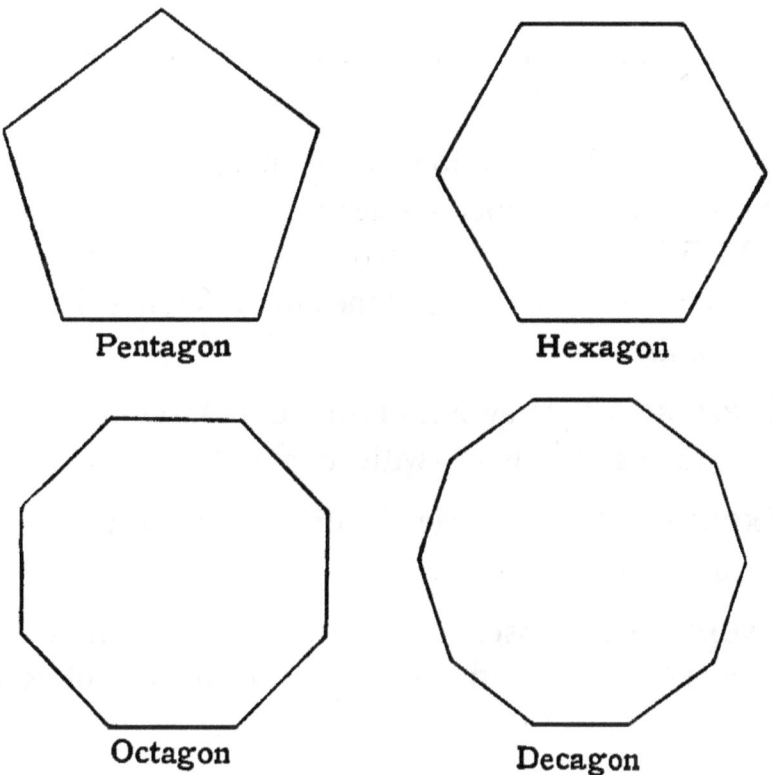

Pentagon   Hexagon

Octagon   Decagon

Exercise 8. What name has been given to a regular figure of *three* sides? What name to a regular figure of *four* sides?

Let us consider a regular pentagon **ABCDE** inscribed in a circle.

Join the centre **O** to each vertex.

How many degrees are there in each of the angles **AOB**, **BOC**, **COD**, **DOE**, **EOA**?

The angle **AOB** is called the **central angle** of the polygon.

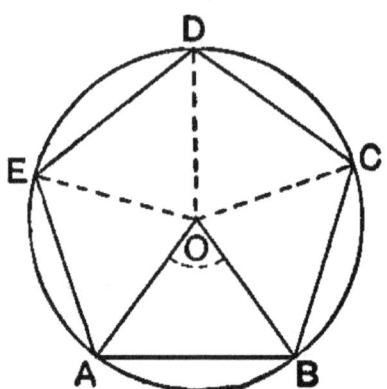

Exercise 9. How many degrees are there in the central angle of (i) an equilateral triangle, (ii) a square, (iii) a regular hexagon, (iv) a regular octagon, (v) a regular decagon?

Which of these angles have you learnt to construct with ruler and compasses only?

It is now evident that to inscribe in a given circle a regular polygon of a given number of sides, we must first draw its *central angle* **AOB**. This fixes the length of the side, or chord, **AB**, which may then be stepped off round the circumference the required number of times.

Exercise 10. Draw a circle of radius 4.5 cm., and inscribe in it an equilateral triangle (with ruler and compasses).

Exercise 11. In a circle of radius 4.5 cm. inscribe a square (with ruler and compasses).

Exercise 12. Inscribe a regular pentagon in a circle of diameter 3.6″ (with protractor). Measure any two of its angles.

Exercise 13. Inscribe a regular hexagon in a circle of radius 1.6″ (with ruler and compasses). Measure any two of its angles.

Join each vertex to the centre, and show by measurements or reasoning that the hexagon consists of *six equilateral triangles.*

Exercise 14. In a circle of diameter 8 cm. inscribe a regular octagon, using your protractor.

Repeat this exercise, using ruler and compasses only.

Exercise 15. Draw a square on a side of 7.0 cm. (with protractor); and find its central point with your ruler.

Draw a circle to pass through all the vertices of the square.

Draw a second circle within the square to touch each of its sides.

Exercise 16. How would you find the central point of an equilateral triangle with ruler and compasses?

Draw an equilateral triangle on a side of 3.0″, and circumscribe a circle about it.

Exercise 17. Draw a circle of radius 1.5″: then draw a square about it, so that each side touches the circle. What is the length of each side?

Exercise 18. *On a side* **AB**, *4 cm. in length, draw a regular* **hexagon**.

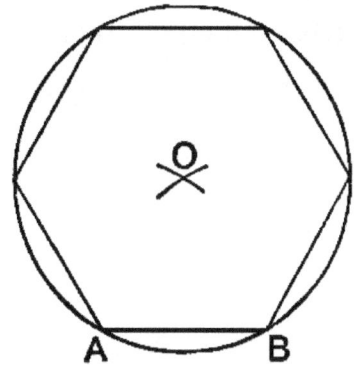

We have seen (Exercise 13) that a regular hexagon is built up of six equilateral triangles, and that its central angle is 60°. This suggests the following construction:

Construction. Find the vertex **O** of an equilateral triangle **AOB**, standing on the base **AB**.

With centre **O** and radius **OA** draw a circle. Then step off chords, each equal to **AB**, round the circumference.

Exercise 19. *On a side* **AB**, *3 cm. in length, draw a regular* **octagon**.

The central angle of a regular octagon is 45°: on this the following construction is based.

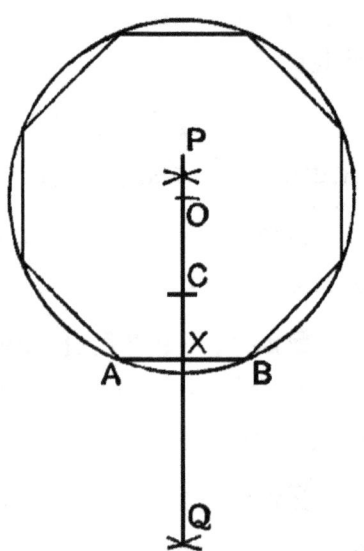

Construction. Bisect **AB** at right angles by the line **PQ**, cutting **AB** at **X**.

From **XP** cut off **XC** equal to **XA**.

From **CP** cut off **CO** equal to **CA**.

With centre **O**, and radius **OA**, draw a circle: then step off chords each equal to **AB** round the circumference.

CIRCLES, POLYGONS

(Verification)

Join **OA**, **OB**. We want to see why the construction makes the ∠ **AOB** equal to 45°. Join **AC**.

How many degrees are there in the ∠ **ACX**, and why?

How many degrees in the ∠ **COA**, and why?

Now deduce the number of degrees in the ∠ **AOB**.

Exercise 20. Show how to cut off the corners of a square so as to obtain from it a regular octagon.

CHAPTER XIV

THE FORM OF SOME SOLID FIGURES

(Rectangular Blocks)

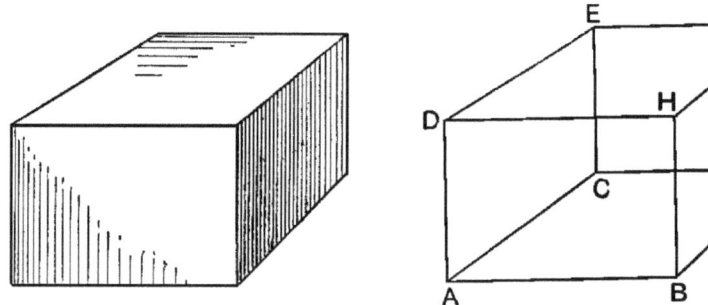

The solid whose shape you are probably most familiar with is that represented by a brick or slab of hewn stone. This solid is called a **rectangular block** or **cuboid**. Let us examine its form more closely.

How many *faces* has it? How many *edges*? How many *corners*, or *vertices*?

The faces are quadrilaterals: of what shape?

Compare two opposite faces. Are they equal? Are they parallel?

SOLID FIGURES, CUBES

We may now sum up our observations thus:

A cuboid has *six* faces; opposite faces being *equal rectangles in parallel planes*. It has *twelve* edges, which fall into three groups, corresponding to the *length*, the *breadth*, and the *height* of the block. The four edges in each group are equal and parallel, and perpendicular to the two faces which they cut.

The length, breadth, and height of a rectangular block are called its **three dimensions**.

Exercise 1. If two dimensions of a rectangular block are equal, say, the breadth **AC** and the height **AD**, two faces take a particular shape. Which faces? What shape?

Exercise 2. If the length, breadth, and height of a rectangular block are all equal, what shapes do the faces take?

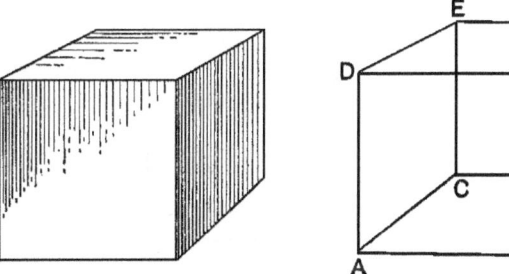

A rectangular block whose length, breadth, and height are all equal is called a **cube**. Its surface consists of six equal squares.

We will now see how models of these solids may be constructed, beginning with the cube, as being the simpler figure.

Suppose the surface of the cube to be cut along the upright edges, and also along the edge **HG**; and suppose the faces to be unfolded and flattened out on the plane of the base. The surface would then be represented by a figure consisting of six squares arranged as below.

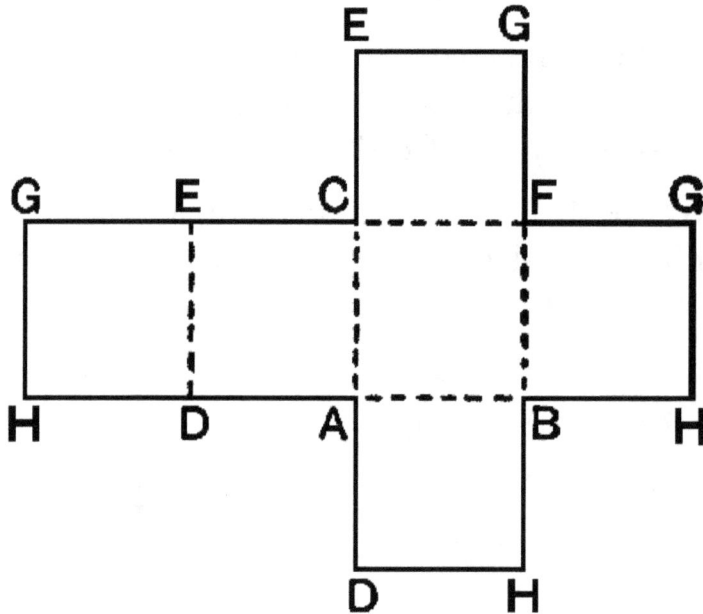

This figure is called the **net** of the cube: it is here drawn on a smaller scale than the cube shown in outline on the previous page.

To make a model of a cube, draw its net on cardboard. Cut out the net along the outside lines, and cut partly through along the dotted lines. Fold the faces over till the edges come together; then fix the edges in position by strips of gummed paper.

Exercise 3. Make a model of a cube each of whose edges is 6.0 cm.

SOLID FIGURES, CUBES

Exercise 4. Make a model of a rectangular block, whose length is 4″, breadth 3″, height 2″.

First draw the net which will consist of six rectangles arranged as below, and having the dimensions marked in the diagram.

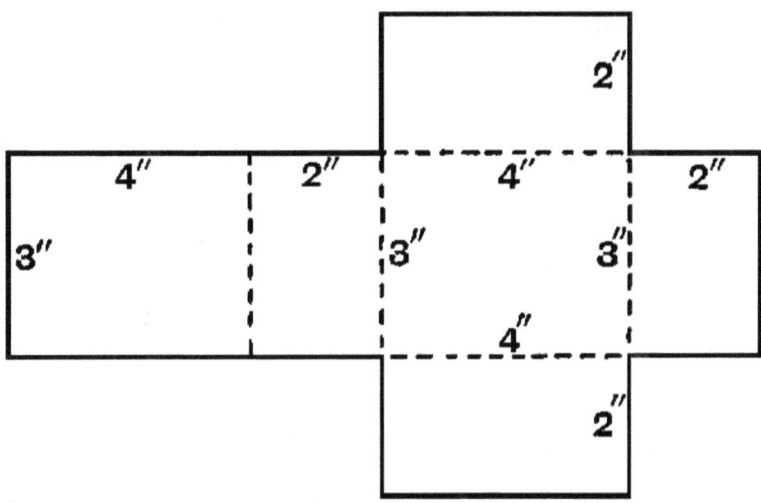

Now cut the net out, fold the faces along the dotted lines, and secure the edges with gummed paper, as already explained.

(Prisms)

Let us now consider a solid whose side-faces (as in a rectangular block) are rectangles, but whose *ends* (i.e. base and top), though equal and parallel, are not necessarily *rectangles* Such a solid is called a **prism**.

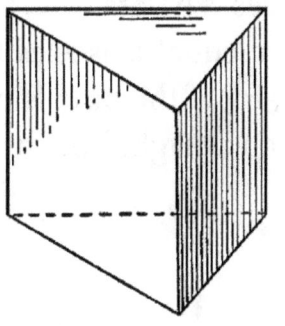 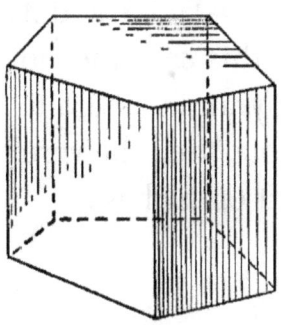

The ends of a prism may be any congruent figures: these may be triangles, quadrilaterals, or polygons of any number of sides. The diagram represents two prisms, one on a triangular base, the other on a pentagonal base.

Exercise 5. Draw the net of a triangular prism, whose ends are equilateral triangles on sides of 5 cm., and whose side-edges measure 7 cm.

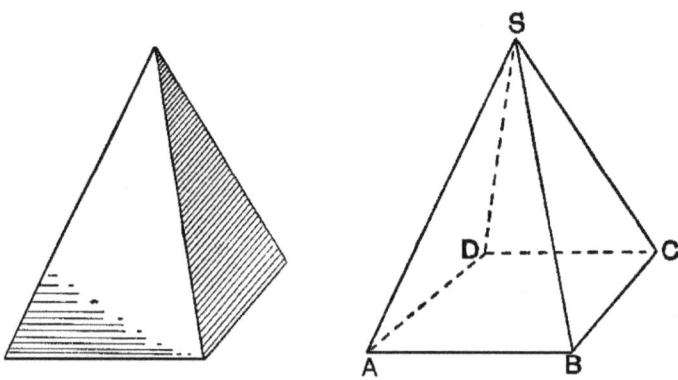

The solid represented in this diagram is called a **pyramid**.

The base of a pyramid (as of a prism) may have any number of sides, but the side-faces must be *triangles* whose vertices are at the same point.

The particular pyramid shown in the Figure stands on a *square* base **ABCD**, and its side-edges **SA**, **SB**, **SC**, **SD** are all equal. In this case the side faces are equal isosceles triangles; and the pyramid is said to be *right*, for if the base is placed on a level table, then the vertex lies in an upright line through the mid-point of the base.

SOLID FIGURES, CUBES

Exercise 6. Make a model of a right pyramid standing on a square base. Each edge of the base is to measure 3″, and each side-edge of the pyramid is to be 4″.

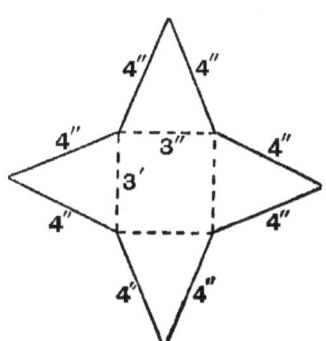

To make the necessary net, draw a square on a side of 3″. This will form the base of the pyramid. Then on the sides of this square draw isosceles triangles making the equal sides in each triangle 4″ long.

Explain why the process of folding about the dotted lines brings the four vertices together.

Another important form of pyramid has as base an equilateral triangle, and all the side edges are equal to the edges of the base.

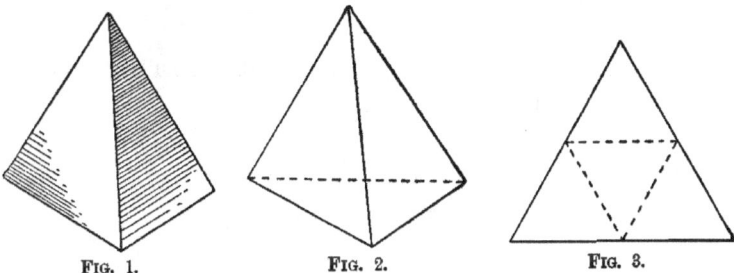

FIG. 1.　　FIG. 2.　　FIG. 3.

How many faces will such a pyramid have? How many edges? What sort of triangles will the side-faces be? Figure 3 shows the net on a reduced scale.

A pyramid of this kind is called a regular **tetrahedron** (from Greek words meaning *four-faced*).

Exercise 7. Construct a model of a regular tetrahedron, each edge of which is 3″ long.

Exercise 8. What is the smallest number of *plane* faces that will enclose a space? What is the smallest number of *curved* surfaces that will enclose a space?

EXPERIMENTAL AND PRACTICAL GEOMETRY

(Cylinders)

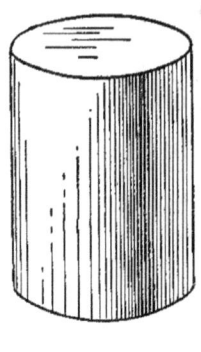
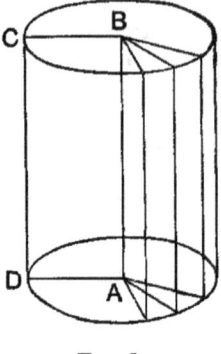

FIG. 1.   FIG. 2.

The solid figure here represented is called a **cylinder**.

On examining the model of which the last diagram is a drawing, you will notice that the two ends are *plane, circular, equal,* and *parallel.*

The side-surface is curved, but not curved in every direction; for it is evidently possible in one direction to rule *straight* lines on the surface: in *what* direction?

Let us take a rectangle **ABCD** (see Figure 2), and suppose it to rotate about one side **AB** as a fixed axis.

What will **BC** and **AD** trace out, as they revolve about **AB**?

Observe that **CD** will move so as always to be parallel to the axis **AB**, and to pass round the curve traced out by **D**. As **CD** moves, it will generate (that is to say, *trace out*) a surface. What sort of surface?

We now see why in *one* direction, namely parallel to the axis **AB**, it is possible to rule *straight* lines on the *curved* surface of a cylinder.

It is easy to find a plane surface to represent the curved surface of a cylinder.

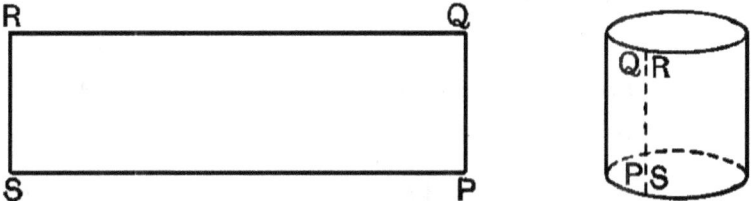

Cut a rectangular strip of paper, making the width **PQ** equal to the height of the cylinder. Wrap the paper round the cylinder, and carefully mark off the length **PS** that will make the paper go exactly once round. Cut off all that overlaps; and then unwrap the covering strip. You have now a rectangle representing the curved surface of the cylinder, and having the same area.

(Cones)

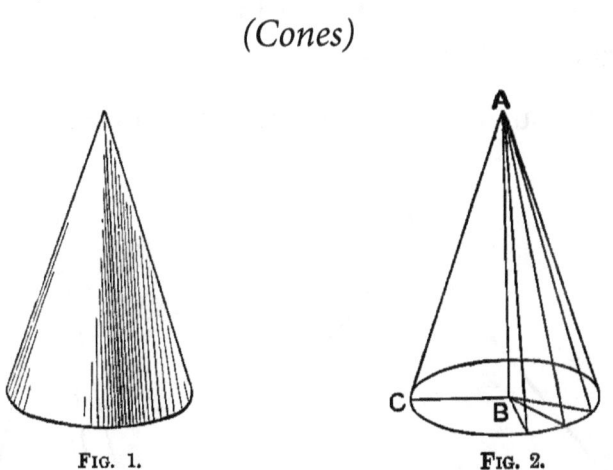

FIG. 1. FIG. 2.

We have now to examine the model of a **cone**, of which a drawing is given above.

Its surface consists of two parts; first a *plane circular* base, then a *curved surface* which tapers from the circumference of the base to a point above it called the vertex. Thus the form of a cone suggests a pyramid standing on a circular instead of a rectilineal base.

Let us take a triangle **ABC** right-angled at **B** (Figure 2), and suppose it to rotate about one side **AB** as a fixed axis. What will **BC** trace out as the triangle revolves? Notice that **AC** will always pass through the *fixed* point **A**, and move round the curve traced out by **C**. As **AC** moves, it will generate a surface. What sort of surface?

We now see that the kind of cone represented in the diagram is a solid generated by the revolution of a right-angled triangle about one side containing the right angle.

Exercise 9. Why must the △ **ABC**, rotating about **AB**, be *right-angled* at **B**, in order to generate a cone?

What would be generated by the revolution of an *obtuse-angled* triangle about one side forming the obtuse angle?

Exercise 10. What would be generated by an *oblique* parallelogram revolving about one side?

The curved surface of a cone may be represented by a plane figure thus:

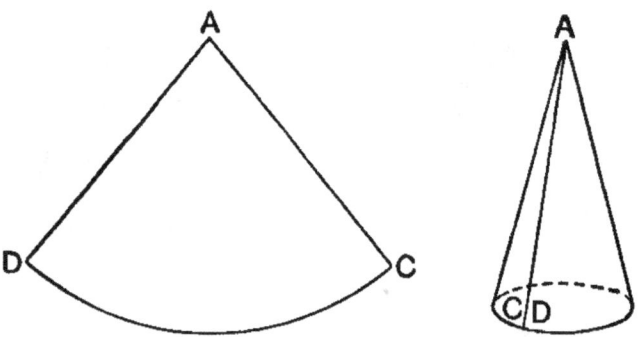

Taking the slant-height **AC** of the cone as radius, draw a circle. Cut it out from your paper; call its centre **A**; and cut it along any radius **AC**. If you now place the centre of the circular paper at the vertex of the cone, you will find that you can wrap the paper round the cone without fold or crease. Mark off from the circumference of your paper the length **CD** that will go

SOLID FIGURES, CUBES

exactly once round the base of the cone; then cut through the radius **AD**. We have now a plane figure **ACD** (called a *sector of a circle*) which represents the curved surface of the cone, and has the same area.

(Spheres)

The last solid we have to consider is the **sphere**, whose shape is that of a globe or billiard ball.

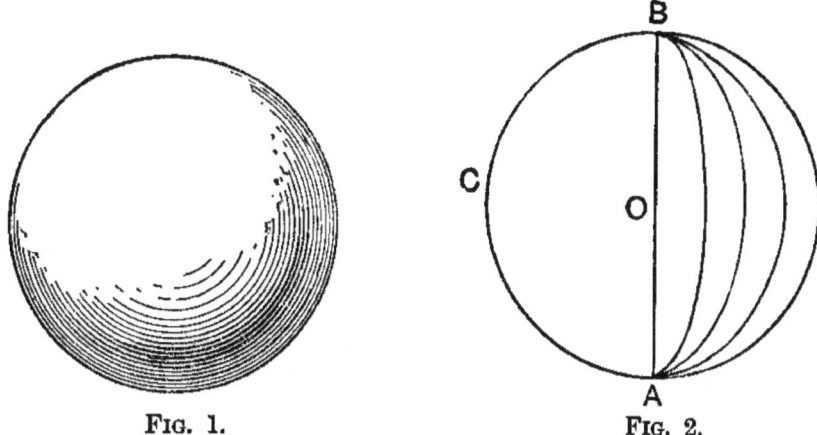

Fig. 1.   Fig. 2.

We shall realise its form more definitely if we imagine a semi-circle **ACB** (Figure 2) to rotate about its diameter as a fixed axis. Then, as the semi-circumference revolves, it generates the surface of a sphere.

Now since all points on the semi-circumference are in all positions at a constant distance from its centre **O**, we see that all points on the surface of a sphere are at a constant distance from a fixed point within it, namely the centre. This constant distance is the radius of the sphere. Thus all straight lines through the centre terminated both ways by the surface are equal: such lines are *diameters*.

Exercise 11. We have seen that on the curved surfaces of a cylinder and cone it is possible (in certain ways only) to rule *straight* lines. Is there any direction in which we can rule a straight line on the surface of a sphere?

Exercise 12. Again we have cut out a *plane* figure that could be wrapped round the *curved* surface of a cylinder without folding, creasing, or stretching. The same has been done for the curved surface of a cone. Can a flat piece of paper be wrapped about a sphere so as to fit all over the surface without creasing?

Exercise 13. Suppose you were to cut a sphere straight through the centre into two parts, in such a way that the new surfaces (made by cutting) are *plane*, these parts would be in every way alike. The parts into which a sphere is divided by a *plane central section* are called hemispheres. Of what shape is the line in which the plane surface meets the curved surface? If the section were *plane* but not *central*, can you tell what the meeting line of the two surfaces would be?

Exercise 14. If a cylinder were cut by a plane parallel to the base, of what shape would the new rim be?

Exercise 15. If a cone were cut by a plane parallel to the base, what would be the form of the section?

ANSWERS

II. MEASUREMENT OF STRAIGHT LINES

1. 1.8″; 3.2″.
2. 4.5 cm.; 8.1 cm.
3. 1.8″; 1.3″; 3.1″.
4. 8.5 cm.; 4.8 cm.; 3.7 cm.
5. 3.0″; 1.2″; 1.1″; 0.7″.
11. 2.54 cm.
15. 400 m.; 560 m.; 80 m.
16. 64 mi.; 4.3″.
17. 22 mi.; 11 mi.; 20 mi.
18. 5 mi.
19. 36 ft.
20. 29 ft.
21. 17 ft.
22. 2½ mi.
23. 31 mi.
24. 50.5 m.

III. STRAIGHT LINES CONTINUED

1. 2.54 cm.
4. **AB** = 1.9″ = 4.8 cm. **CD** = 3.2″ = 8.2 cm.
   EF = 1.2″ = 3.0 cm. **GH** = 4.4″ = 11.1 cm.
6. 2.83″; 2.12″; 1.41″; 0.70″.

IV. CIRCLES

13. P is 2.5″ from **A** and from **B**. Q is 2″ from **A** and from **B**.
14. Two; one on each side of **AB**.   15. Two.   16. Two.
22. About 2.1″.

V. ANGLES

7. 90°, 180°, 270°, 360°.

8. 30°, 150°, 216°.   8 min., 17 min., 1½ min.

9. 60°.

10. 45°, 90°, 135°, 180°.

11. 30°, 60°, 90°, 120°, 150°, 180°.   60°, 60°.

22. (i) 115°; (ii) 40°; (iii) 27°.

25. (i) $\angle$ **BOC** = 37°, $\angle$ **COA** = 143°, $\angle$ **AOD** = 37°.

(ii) $\angle$ **DOB** = 151°, $\angle$ **BOC** = 29°, $\angle$ **COA** = 151°.

(iii) $\angle$ **BOD** = 137°, $\angle$ **DOA** = 43°, $\angle$ **COB** = 43°.

28. (i) 153°; (ii) 74°.

VII. DIRECTION, PARALLELS

18. 7.8 km.

19. 390 yds.

20. 9.9 km.

21. 10 mi.

22. About 30½ mi. N. 25° W.

23. 630 yds.

24. 3 km.

VIII. PERPENDICULARS

1. 6 cm.

5. On the perpendicular bisector of **AB**.   Two.

7. A square.

8. 4.8 cm.

10. (a) A square. (b) A square. 90°. (c) 90°.

17. 1.5″.

ANSWERS

IX. TRIANGLES

10. 45°.

11. $a = 12$ cm., **B** = 35°, **C** = 27°.

14. 50°. $b = c = 2.86''$. (i) Isosceles, (ii) acute-angled.

15. 84°. $a = 5.5$ cm., $c = 3.6$ cm.

17. 30°.

X. TRIANGLES CONTINUED

14. ∠ **AXB** = 73°; ∠ **AXC** = 107°.
16. 30°.
17. 30°. 12.5 cm.
27. 430 yds.
28. E. 37° N.
29. No, by about 0.1 of a mile.
30. 134 ft.
31. 31°
32. 683 yds.
33. 162 metres.
34. 505 ft.
35. Due North.
36. 159 yds.
37. Nearly 17 mi.
38. 150 yds.
39. 566 yds.; 400 yds.
40. About 32 mi.
41. 132 ft.
42. 20 ft.
43. 12 ft.
44. Nearly 300 metres.

XI. QUADRILATERALS

5. ∠ **ABC** = 58°, ∠ **BCD** = 122°, ∠ **ADC** = 58°.
7. The square and rectangle.
9. 3.5″.
10. 2.1″.
11. 5 cm.
14. Five.
15. 60 metres. N.W.
16. 19.1 cm.
17. 175 yds.

XII. AREAS

1. 180.

2. (i) 200; (ii) 180; (iii) 200; (iv) 80.

4. (ii) has an area of 72 squares,
   (v) an area of 78½ squares;
   each of the other figures has an area of 80 squares.

5. 100.

6. Four.

7. (i) Three. (ii) Nine. (iii) Six.

9. 200 sq. ft.

10. 1 sq. yd.   375 sq. yds.

11. (i) 180; (ii) 400; (iii) 900; (iv) 200; (v) 20.

12. 2″.

13. Breadth = 4 cm.

14. 1.6″.

15. 64 sq. ft.

16. 100 sq. ft.; 2000 sq. ft.

17. 1200 sq. ft.

18. 125 sq. mi.

19. 625 sq. yds.

20. 40 yds.; 2000 sq. yds.

21. 120 squares.

24. 5 sq. in.

25. 36 sq. cm.

26. 1.53″; 2.06 sq. in.

27. 28 sq. in.

28. 5.7 cm.; 45.6 sq. cm.

29. 6 sq. in.; 3 sq. in.

31. 20 sq. cm.

35. 4800 sq. yds.

36. Each = 1296 sq. m.

37. 1.73 sq. in.

38. 20.3 sq. cm.

39. 22.9 sq. cm.

ANSWERS

XIII. MISCELLANEOUS CONSTRUCTIONS

4. 5.0 cm.

5. 2.0″.

6. Each tangent = 9.6 cm.

7. A rhombus.

8. Equilateral △. Square.

9. (i) 120°; (ii) 90°; (iii) 60°; (iv) 45°; (v) 36°.

12. 108°.

13. 120°.

17. 3.0″.

XIV. SOLID FIGURES

1. The opposite faces **ACED**, **BFGH** are squares.

2. Each face is a square.

8. Four. Two.

9. A cone with a conical cavity at one end.

10. A cylinder with a conical cavity at one end and a conical peak at the other.

11. No.

12. No.

13. A circle. A circle.

14. A circle. A circle.

www.ingramcontent.com/pod-product-compliance
Lightning Source LLC
Chambersburg PA
CBHW080515110426
42742CB00017B/3121